True Songs of Freedom

True Songs of Freedom

Uncle Tom's Cabin
in Russian Culture and Society

John MacKay

THE UNIVERSITY OF WISCONSIN PRESS

This book was published with the assistance of the
FREDERICK W. HILLES PUBLICATION FUND
of Yale University

The University of Wisconsin Press
1930 Monroe Street, 3rd Floor
Madison, Wisconsin 53711-2059
uwpress.wisc.edu

3 Henrietta Street
London WC2E 8LU, England
eurospanbookstore.com

Library of Congress Cataloging-in-Publication Data

MacKay, John (John Kenneth)
    True songs of freedom : Uncle Tom's cabin in Russian culture
    and society / John MacKay.
        p.   cm.
    Includes bibliographical references and index.
    ISBN 978-0-299-29294-2 (pbk.: alk. paper)
    ISBN 978-0-299-29293-5 (e-book)
    1. Stowe, Harriet Beecher, 1811–1896. Uncle Tom's cabin.
    2. Stowe, Harriet Beecher, 1811–1896—Appreciation—Russia.
    3. Stowe, Harriet Beecher, 1811–1896—Influence.
    4. Stowe, Harriet Beecher, 1811–1896—Translations into Russian—History and criticism.
    5. Russia—Intellectual life—19th century.
    6. Russia—Intellectual life—20th century.
    7. Soviet Union—Intellectual life.   I. Title.
    PS2954.U6M26 2013
    813'.3—dc23
    2012032683

To

MOIRA

Contents

Illustrations

Acknowledgments

This book took a while to reach completion, partially because it was a lot of fun to write.

As usual, everyone at the University of Wisconsin Press was terrific. My heartiest thanks to Matthew Cosby, Frances Grogan, Sheila Leary, Carla Marolt, Adam Mehring, Barbara Wojhoski, Logan Middleton, Lauren Vedal, and especially Gwen Walker for all the help and support. I'm very grateful to Sarah Meer, Nancy Ruttenburg, and the anonymous reviewers for their enormously useful suggestions.

For their advice, great ideas, research help, and encouragement, a big thank-you to Vladimir Alexandrov, Amanda Brickell Bellows, David Blight, Paul Bushkovitch, Hazel Carby, Katerina Clark, Michael Denning, Wai Chee Dimock, Irina Dolgova, Laura Engelstein, Masha Etkind, Harvey Goldblatt, Irina Golubchikov (and Liuda and Lyosha), Bella Grigoryan, Joan Hedrick, Julia Herzberg, Fredric Jameson, Dennis Jones, Liza Knapp, Sergei Kudriavtsev, Sarah Lewis, David Moon, Charles Musser, David Reynolds, Natalie Ryabchikova, Benjamin Schenk, Laurence Senelick, Maria Sidorkina, Timothy Snyder, Willard Sunderland, Tomas Venclova, Laura Wexler, Susan Willis, and Emily Yao.

As always, I lift a glass to my wonderful colleagues in Yale's Department of Slavic Languages and Literatures and Film Studies Program, my comrades in the Working Group in Marxism and Cultural Theory, and all my students in the various iterations of the "American slavery and Russian serfdom" course over the years. Another special thanks to Denise Kohn, Sarah Meer, and Emily B. Todd, who saw my earliest work on Stowe in Russia to publication.

A lot of research went into this short book, none of which would have been possible without the help of the staff at Yale's Sterling and Beinecke Libraries, and especially at the National Library of Russia in St. Petersburg and the State Library of the Russian Federation in Moscow. Archival research was carried out at my beloved Russian State Archive of Literature and Art (RGALI) in Moscow: deepest thanks to Tatiana Goriaeva, Galina Zlobina, and my dear friends Dmitri Neustroev and Elena Tchougounova. Generous research funding from Yale's Whitney Humanities Center supported my work in Russia.

Time spent in Moscow wouldn't be nearly as delightful as it always is without Anya Petanova, Marina Evgenieva, Sonya, Stasia, and Tim; I toast you all.

I'm extraordinarily lucky to enjoy the loving support of my family: my parents Jack and Betty MacKay, my sister Pam, my brother Peter, and their families. Thanks, too, to all the folks in Argentina.

As it turns out, the very first public performance of tango in Argentina took place during a staging of *Uncle Tom's Cabin* in Buenos Aires in 1856 (http://www.protangoperu.com/investigacion/evolucion.html). I was unable to fit this detail anywhere into the book; for Moira Fradinger, to whom the book is dedicated, I include it here.

Historical Timeline

20 March 1852	Harriet Beecher Stowe's *Uncle Tom's Cabin* first published in book form
1853–56	Crimean War
End of 1857	First publications of *Uncle Tom's Cabin* in Russia
1861–65	US Civil War
19 February 1861	Emancipation of Russia's serfs by Tsar Alexander II
1865–77	Reconstruction Era in the United States
13 March 1881	Assassination of Tsar Alexander II
1891–92	Major famine in Russian countryside
1896	*Plessy v. Ferguson* Supreme Court decision, upholding the rights of states to impose laws enforcing racial segregation in the United States
1 July 1896	Death of Harriet Beecher Stowe
1905–7	First Russian Revolution; termination of "redemption payments" paid by former serf households (1907)
1914–18	World War 1
February 1917	February Revolution; abdication of Tsar Nicholas II
October 1917	October Revolution; seizure of power by Vladimir Lenin's Bolshevik Party
1918–21	Russian Civil War
1922	Formation of the Soviet Union
21 January 1924	Death of Lenin
1920s–1930s	Period of the journeys of "black pilgrims" from the United States to the USSR
1928	Joseph Stalin consolidates power; beginning of First Five-Year Plan

1929	Beginning of violent drive to collectivize all agriculture in the USSR; results in colossal famine that kills millions in 1932–33; beginning of Great Depression
1930	Beginning of Stalin-era forced labor camp (gulag) system
1932	Dissolution of existing Soviet artistic organizations; formation of official Unions of Soviet Artists
1933	United States inaugurates diplomatic relations with the Soviet Union; Hitler comes to power in Germany
1934–39	Popular Front period
1936	Margaret Mitchell publishes *Gone with the Wind*
1936–38	Great Terror
1939	Treaty of nonaggression between Germany and the Soviet Union
1941–45	Great Patriotic War (Nazi-Soviet War); over 25 million Soviet citizens die
1947–62	Peak years of the Cold War
1948	Founding of the State of Israel; beginnings of Stalin-era anti-Semitic (anticosmopolitan) campaign
1949	James Baldwin publishes "Everybody's Protest Novel" in *Partisan Review*
1950–53	Korean War
5 March 1953	Death of Stalin
1954	*Brown v. Board of Education* Supreme Court decision overturns *Plessy v. Ferguson*, declares segregation of public schools unconstitutional
1955	Beginning of Vietnam War (ends 1975)
1956	Soviet invasion of Hungary; beginnings of the Khrushchev-era cultural and political "thaw"; ends with Nikita Khrushchev's replacement by Leonid Brezhnev in 1964
First half of 1960s	Emergence of anti-Soviet dissidence in the USSR
October 1962	Cuban Missile Crisis
22 November 1963	Assassination of John F. Kennedy
1968	Soviet suppression of Prague Spring in Czechoslovakia; assassination of Martin Luther King, Jr.
1971–79	Soviet-US détente, followed by the "Second Cold War" (through 1985)
1973	Beginning of Brezhnev-era economic stagnation

1985	Mikhail Gorbachev elected secretary of the Communist Party of the USSR; beginning of perestroika and glasnost
1991	Dissolution of the Soviet Union, Russia becomes independent country; Gorbachev replaced by Boris Yeltsin; severe economic downturn through the end of the decade
1999	Vladimir Putin replaces Yeltsin

True Songs of Freedom

Introduction

I'm reading now, for the first time in my life, *Uncle Tom's Cabin*
in its entirety. An excellent book, courageous and completely
contemporary. I read Feuchtwanger's *Jud Süss*: also contemporary. All offenses, all injuries—they're as old as the world.
    Marina Tsvetaeva, *Sobranie sochinenij v semi tomakh*

Since childhood I've loved American writers. I felt agitated delight when reading Edgar Allan Poe, I laughed over Bret Harte,
I love Mark Twain with the devoted, fraternal love of a school-
boy, just as all Soviet children love him. . . . I have to admit that
the only one I didn't love was Stowe. Her sentimentality and
piety struck me as dissimulation. A porcelain statuette of a
weeping pug stood on a table at my grandmother's house—as
children we called this pug "somebody reading Stowe."
    Konstantin Paustovsky, "Novoe pokolenie
    amerikanskikh pisatelej"

M Y TWO EPIGRAPHS, drawn from occasional comments by two
major twentieth-century Russian writers, represent not the full
range but rather the extreme antipodes of Russian and Russo-Soviet
opinion surrounding Harriet Beecher Stowe's legendary antislavery
novel *Uncle Tom's Cabin* (1852).[1] The first comes from a letter of 10
November 1938 written by Marina Tsvetaeva (1892–1941) to her Czech
friend Anna Tesková (1872–1954).[2] Tsvetaeva, one of the greatest European lyric poets of the twentieth century, was writing in the midst of
terrible personal and historical crisis. In Parisian exile since 1925, she
had endured years of poverty-stricken isolation, a victim of émigré

3

intrigues and social ostracism. Soon after the letter was written, she would follow her husband, Sergei Efron, and daughter Ariadna back to Stalin's Soviet Union, where in 1939 both husband and daughter would be arrested and tortured (and Sergei eventually shot) and where, on 31 August 1941, she would hang herself in utter solitude, two months after the Nazis invaded Soviet territory.[3] But the letter is shadowed by a more immediate anxiety about her addressee's situation: less than two months before the letter was written, the Czechoslovak government had disastrously surrendered (on 30 September 1938) to Nazi Germany as part of the notorious Munich Agreement.[4] Past suffering and a sense of imminent catastrophe inform Tsvetaeva's letter, which would be among the last she would send to her friend in Prague.[5]

Tsvetaeva is known for her vivid prose evocations of childhood and (especially) childhood reading, but although *Uncle Tom's Cabin* had become a "children's book" for many by this time (in Russia and elsewhere), the poet receives the book as grown up in every sense: "completely contemporary" here must mean "fully adult" as well as "entirely relevant." Plainly, her mention of *Jud Süss* (1925) implies a comparison between the suffering protagonists of Stowe's novel—Uncle Tom, but surely Eliza and perhaps others as well—and Lion Feuchtwanger's hero Josef Süss Oppenheimer, martyred at the hands of anti-Semites at the novel's end. The topicality of this last allusion is in no doubt whatsoever, for Tsvetaeva was writing the day after the Kristallnacht pogroms had swept across Germany—a country whose language, literature, and culture the poet deeply knew and dearly loved—in a wave of terror against Jews often regarded as the inaugural moment of the Holocaust. This event (9–10 November 1938)—which spread to the recently Nazi-occupied Czechoslovakian territory called the Sudetenland—surely offered the most immediate occasion for Tsvetaeva's comments.[6]

Her reference to *Uncle Tom's Cabin*, by contrast, has a universalizing function, serving to extend the sense of present "offense and injury" over a broader historical and geographical field. Yet Tsvetaeva's description of Stowe's book as "courageous" (*muzhestvennaia*, which might just as easily be translated as "manly" or "steadfast") also implies that this is a book with strength—not just "brave" in terms of the stand it takes but able to make its readers brave as well. Perhaps Tsvetaeva was unaware of *Uncle Tom's* reputation for self-indulgent "feminine" weepiness; in any case, her typically creative coupling of an adjective with masculine connotations (*muzhestvennaia* carries echoes of *muzh* [husband], *muzhchina* [man], and similar cognates) with the (grammatically) feminine *kniga* (book) cuts through the usual clichés to fashion a casually androgynous image of writerly defiance: a *"muzhestvennaia kniga."*[7] At the same time, of course, the universalizing gesture (victimization is "as old as the world") carries a recognizably Tsvetaevan tone of melancholy and even fatalism, attitudes that inform the sense of "Tsvetaeva" we derive from the poetry, early and late. As both poet and woman, Tsvetaeva lived much of her life on the margins and sought imaginative, supportive analogies for that marginality in more collective and historical kinds of exclusion, as most famously here in the great *Poem of the End* (*Poema kontsa*) of 1924:

Life is a place where it's forbidden
    to live. Like the Hebrew quarter.

And isn't it more worthy to
    become an eternal Jew?
Anyone not a reptile
    suffers the same pogrom.

[. . .]

Ghetto of the chosen. Beyond this
    ditch. No mercy
In this most Christian of worlds
    all poets are [Yids].[8]

In a different context, with a different example of mass exclusion at hand, might she (also) have written that all poets are Uncle Toms, or Elizas?

The second epigraph comes from a brief essay by Konstantin Paustovsky (1898–1968), an important Soviet author of stories, novels, plays and memoirs, most famous for his autobiographical *Story of a Life* (1945–63). A master of lyrical prose in the Anton Chekhov–Ivan Bunin tradition, Paustovsky both managed to work (and survive) through the Stalin period and succeeded in maintaining a certain creative distance from official socialist-realist norms. Engaged after 1956, during the post-Stalin "thaw," with introducing new and formerly suppressed authors to the Soviet public, he won the respect of many young people through his open and courageous defense of dissident figures like writers Andrei Sinyavsky and Yuli Daniel.[9] Paustovsky's career was, in short, as great a success as Tsvetaeva's was, in virtually every external sense, a failure.

His remark on Stowe (clearly he's speaking about *Uncle Tom's Cabin*) was written in the 1960s and appeared in a Cold War-era collection of

Russian and Soviet responses to US writing. The evaluation of Stowe's novel could not be more unlike Tsvetaeva's, of course; yet a closer look at Paustovsky's words reveals a similar tension between particular occasion and universal claim, here displaced to a different level. The particular (unspoken) occasion is the Cold War itself, and part of Paustovsky's job in his article is to define and delimit his own literary relationship to "America." That relationship is both positive and laden with emotion—anxious delight, laughter, love—but *Uncle Tom's Cabin* marks the border of Paustovsky's affection. This limit is justified (and here's where the "universal" comes in) by a strategic appeal to childhood experience. Inverting in a different way the book's status as "children's literature," Paustovsky's children are natural masters, like the child who sees the notoriously unclothed emperor, of Brechtian *plumpes Denken* (crude thought); untrammeled by adult pieties or "sentimental education," they are able, unlike their grandmother, to distinguish true from fabricated emotionality. Indeed, Paustovsky implies that Stowe's book is itself somehow "childish" or immature, inasmuch as it (like Grandmother's weeping pug) belongs to an earlier, superseded childhood of taste. If the word "kitsch" had been available to Paustovsky, he probably would have used it.[10]

The two authors' comments can be used to demarcate (not exhaustively, to be sure) a dialectical field of possible responses to Stowe's novel. Tsvetaeva has no doubt about the book's contemporary relevance and persistent strength, but that strength hypertrophies, on her account, to the point where the novel's protagonists verge on becoming universal types for equally universal suffering and victimization, rather than prompts to action—archetypes, not instigations. Paustovsky for his part also senses strength in *Uncle Tom's Cabin*, but regards it as dependent on a time-bound and mechanical rhetoric and therefore essentially closed off from any authentic relation to readers or the world. The danger of his response lies in the categorical nature of the dismissal, which looks suspiciously like contempt: children are not always wise, and their laughter and the pug's porcelain tears end up mirroring each other in their isolation. What is clear is that both writers regard *Uncle Tom's Cabin* as a book with power; how that power is articulated, and how those articulations are to be assessed, is the controversial matter.

Uncle Tom's Cabin; or, Life among the Lowly, the nineteenth century's best-selling novel globally, has long been regarded as one of the most important books ever published by an American author. At its center are the stories of two black slaves—the bold and beautiful quadroon

Eliza and the simple, strong and Christlike Uncle Tom—the first of whom escapes bondage with her husband and son, while the second dies a martyr at the whim of his brutal owner.[11] Originally a major focal point for discussions of slavery in the pre–Civil War United States, and the target of ferocious denunciation (sometimes in the form of "anti-*Tom*" novels) from Southern proslavery ideologues who regarded its depiction of bondage as false and/or dangerous, *Uncle Tom's Cabin*, whether encountered as novel, play, film, or otherwise, has nearly from its first appearance provoked controversy about its proposed solutions to the slavery problem (particularly its concluding suggestion that freed blacks be sent back to Africa to colonize Liberia); about its literary quality or lack thereof (and by extension, about what criteria might be used for evaluating politically engaged literature as such); about its apparent susceptibility to the crassest commercial exploitation; and not least about its representations of black people (especially the long-suffering Uncle Tom, whose name had become an "epithet of servility" by the 1960s) and the structuring presence within it of nineteenth-century ideologies of white racial superiority.[12] An explosion of scholarly writing since the late 1970s, much of it framed by the reevaluation of sentiment as a political strategy by US feminist critics, has repositioned *Uncle Tom's Cabin* as a central object of theoretical and historical inquiry at the intersection of the most vexing questions about race, gender, the affective and political character of reading, and literary and cultural history.[13] Despite (and also because of) this extraordinary critical and historical work, *Uncle Tom's Cabin* remains a challenging text, as anyone who has had to teach it can verify.

Uncle Tom's Cabin elicited countless intense and complex responses around the world, of course, although (with the exception of the relatively well-researched British reception) we still know too little about the specifics of those responses, especially in non-English-speaking countries.[14] This represents a significant gap in scholarship, given both the book's broad dissemination and its power to provoke considerations of racial representation, women's writing, literature and politics, and attitudes toward the United States, among other topics. While alluding occasionally to other national receptions for purposes of comparison and clarification, the present book confines itself to the responses to *Uncle Tom's Cabin* in Russia (including the Russian-speaking segment of the Soviet Union [1922–91]), a country with a particularly complex long-term relationship not only to Stowe's novel but to rural bondage and its legacies, to the issue of the political efficacy of literature, to the United States, and to questions of democracy, equality, resistance, and freedom.

Uncle Tom's Cabin—in Russian, *Khízhina diádi Tóma*—was published in at least sixty-seven different editions in Russia between 1857 and 1917; well over seventy separate editions in at least twenty-one different languages appeared in the Soviet Union between 1925 and 1991.[15] By the early twentieth century, it had become a classic of world literature for Russians and was a ubiquitous feature (usually in variously cut or otherwise altered versions) of the childhood reading of Soviet citizens, especially in the post–World War 2 period, during which time at least three million copies rolled off presses in the USSR.[16] Though not without significant gaps, the story of the novel's reception overlaps with 150 years of a history as tumultuous as that of any nation on earth during the same period. Appearing in Russian three years prior to the statutory abolition of serfdom, in the postemancipation period *Uncle Tom's Cabin* became both an educational tool and a touchstone for the Russian (and later Russo-Soviet) educated elite's sense of its own identity and values.

This study of *Uncle Tom's Cabin's* Russian reception is parsed into five clearly historically demarcated divisions: the period before and around the time of the first publication in Russian in 1857/58; significant responses to the novel from (roughly) 1858 to 1917; the early Soviet period (1922–45); the Cold War through to 1991; and a coda on the post-Soviet context. Clearly, it is impossible to provide an exhaustive account of such a lengthy and many-faceted reception in a brief account like this one. Much has been left out, whether for the sake of economy or (more regrettably) out of ignorance, and much work remains to be done. The readers I focus on are for the most part well-known figures (such as Alexander Herzen, Nikolai Chernyshevsky, Ivan Turgenev, and Leo Tolstoy), whose responses to *Uncle Tom's Cabin* have been preserved in letters, diaries, and essays, and who helped condition the way the novel has been read in Russia generally.

By contrast, little will be said here about how the book has been received by "ordinary" readers; reliable data on *this* reception is scarce indeed, and the best I can do is shape some sense of what it might have been like by focusing on the channels through which the novel was propagated: prefaces, articles, and above all the translations themselves.[17] What I do hope to achieve is, on the one hand, typical for studies of this kind: to test the effects of context and history upon reception, certainly, but also to see the book in a fresh way, as the prism of that "other" reception that brings new aspects and unexpected problems to light.

Indeed, although I discuss Russian social, literary, and publishing history throughout, I see this book (perversely perhaps) as primarily a study of *Uncle Tom's Cabin*—even a close reading of sorts, but executed as if through a multifaceted crystal, turning on its axes.[18]

Thus, my main protagonists will be members of Russia's educated elites—including creative writers and polemicists of conservative, moderate, or radical cast—moving across the media landscape in which they conversed and debated: overwhelmingly, though not exclusively, a landscape of print and written script, including everything from personal letters to encyclopedia entries.[19] Tracing the fortunes of *Uncle Tom's Cabin* in Russia enables us to chart out a microepisode in the "spiritual life" of those elites. Of varying political persuasions, they insisted on partitioning discourse and the kinds of work performed on discourse in specific ways—for instance, holding "art" apart from "social engagement" or demanding their coordination or fusion; distinguishing (or not) the sphere of ethics from that of religion—and were thus all pedagogues or even "enlighteners" at core, who took the printed word and its potential effects, especially upon newly literate readers, very seriously.[20] A book as popular, as unstable in literary reputation, and as ideologically fraught as *Uncle Tom's Cabin* could not but attract the attention of those enlighteners (and counterenlighteners), especially starting around the 1880s, when a truly mass reading public began to emerge in Russia.[21]

The original impulse to publish a Russian *Uncle Tom's Cabin* had come from the ranks of the educated elite; indeed, even prior to the novel's appearance in Russian, and despite all efforts by the authorities, many members of Russia's literate public of the 1850s read it as an allegorical attack on and description of Russia's own serfdom-based society. In what follows, I hope to show how *Uncle Tom's Cabin* prompted members of that public to engage in a fascinating comparative reflection upon their own society and that of the distant United States through the prism of bondage. Encountering Stowe's novel in an atmosphere of constraint—the book was banned in Russia until late 1857—Russian intellectuals at home and abroad nonetheless responded to it in remarkably diverse ways that reflected the full range of Russian views on politics and literature, the elite and the peasantry, Russia and its "others."

The case of *Uncle Tom* shows how Russian thinkers disagreed about the very "comparability" of their society to any other, with conservatives (like the Slavophile Alexei Khomyakov) arguing strongly for national specificity, and radicals (like Alexander Herzen) insisting on the relevance of Stowe's novel to Russian conditions. At the same time, and paradoxically, some of those who sought analogies between their own Russia and Stowe's South feared that the overwhelming affective force of *Uncle Tom* would draw world attention away from the scandal of Russian bondage rather than generating the required global abolitionism. These early readers, as we will see, were continually trying to reconcile the book's analytical force—its critical exposure of the structure of master-slave relations—with its "sentimental power," to unite those energies in a way that could be applied to the Russian predicament. Broadening the historical frame, we can also see, in retrospect at least, how the educated elites were already involved through these readings in conceptualizing a national culture or "symbolic unity" for Russia, not unlike elites in other countries.[22] Thus it may not be surprising that their minds were drawn into imaginings of another society deeply structured by bondage and its legacies, another continental empire.[23]

Although *Uncle Tom's Cabin* predictably lost its sharp topicality after the emancipation, it became important starting in the 1880s as a widely distributed pedagogic novel of Christian example, with Uncle Tom presented as a model—especially for children and peasants—of piety, probity, and calm strength of conviction. I hope to show that in the forty years prior to the 1917 revolution, *Uncle Tom's Cabin* became a kind of quilting point for different kinds of audiences, markets, and values, thus giving us a small glimpse into some of the conditions of possibility enabling the emergence of a Russian reading public that would extend far beyond the elites.

For its part, the very different culture that emerged in the aftermath of the October Revolution received Stowe's novel in particularly fraught and complex ways. To be sure, the tension between the book's critique of exploitation and its strong religious pathos opened up new contradictions of response; at the same time, *Uncle Tom's Cabin* came to be even more intensively instrumentalized than previously, both as a source of knowledge about the United States and its racist social structure, and as anticapitalist and anti-US propaganda. Thus the Soviet reception, in particular, offers useful insights into the contradictions of what today would be called "human rights discourse," as that discourse is inflected by geopolitical imperatives and hegemonic aspirations within the realm of culture (here, "literature").

The "local" history that I trace here will, I hope, prove to be of more general comparative interest as well, especially insofar as Stowe's own milieu in America was very much a crusading and "civilizing" one, and later US discussions of the novel also tended to center on its effects as a source of values and exempla.[24] The extraordinary worldwide dissemination and complex reputation of *Uncle Tom's Cabin* should make it a disconcertingly prominent exhibit in the gallery of "world literature"; the case of *Uncle Tom* in Russia demonstrates that the layout and perimeters of that gallery should be decided via direct consideration of the literate publics that sustain it, whether thought of as (always unstable) national or local readerships, or across a more global canvas: "comparative elites and readerships" bound to "comparative literature."

Although I am unable to make any large-scale or fine-grained sociological comparisons here, we will see that the reading publics, and especially the educated elites, in the United States and Russia (and elsewhere) posed similar questions to *Uncle Tom's Cabin*. Is this a book with a humanizing and edifying effect or a coarsening and reifying one; how can one understand a work that has been read at once as a moral classic of humanity, a sacred text, the example par excellence of an effective *litterature engagée,* a piece of racist kitsch, and "the World's Greatest Hit"?[25] In what follows, I explore some of the Russian answers to these questions.

1

Before Emancipation

It isn't so in Vermont.
    Miss Ophelia

TSAR ALEXANDER II officially abolished serfdom in Russia on 19 February 1861, thus freeing circa twenty-two million men, women, and children (or over 35 percent of the entire population of the country) from the approximately one hundred thousand nobles who owned them. Although historians have argued that the actual abolition process began long before and ended long after this date, we can for convenience's sake take it as the pivotal moment in the history of the disappearance of this form of chattel slavery.[1] In the years leading up to the proclamation, there was, of course, no "sectional" journalistic polemic in Russia of the type that helped give birth to *Uncle Tom's Cabin*: no North from which to launch abolitionist attacks on bondage, no South where proslavery thought might be nurtured and propagated. Under conditions of absolute monarchy, the degree of government interference with the press (in the form of censorship) was markedly greater in Russia than in the United States, and the number of actual journalistic organs considerably smaller.[2] The "peasant question" had been a topic of concern, however, since the late eighteenth century, with salons, government committee meetings, private oral or epistolary exchanges, and secret societies as the main settings for debate. And some writing openly or obliquely critical of serfdom did appear even before Alexander's accession to the throne in 1855, after which time one can detect a certain softening in restrictions on the press, though hardly a full-scale relaxation.[3] What is clear (from a comparative angle) is that the amount of Russian print devoted from whatever perspective to the question of bondage was, by US standards, very small indeed.[4]

Already by 1857, *Uncle Tom's Cabin* had appeared in Armenian (1854; published in Venice), Czech (1854), Danish (1853), Dutch (1853), Finnish (1856), Flemish (1852), French (eleven different translations, and more editions, in the space of ten months in 1852–53), German (at least twenty-nine editions in 1852–53), Hungarian (thrice: 1853,1856,1857), Italian (1853), Polish (1853), Portuguese (a Parisian edition from 1853), Slovene (1853), Spanish (six 1853 editions, published in Mexico, Bogotá, and Madrid), Romanian (1853), and Welsh (1853).[5] This dissemination, extraordinary by any standards and probably of greater scope than my sources indicate, helped to make the novel a point of reference for discussions of bondage internationally in the 1850s. But *Uncle Tom's Cabin* had to wait until very late in 1857 to appear in Russian, although it was (as we will see later) already familiar to many in intellectual circles, usually in French or German translation. The relative lateness of the Russian version (given the rapid early proliferation of translations) has led some to guess that the book's publication had hitherto been banned.[6] And although we have no actual written record of an official prohibition, there is indeed some evidence, negative and positive, of suppression.

Journals of all political stripes made it a practice in the 1850s to do overviews of the literary/cultural scenes in Western Europe, and particularly those of Paris and London. Yet no substantive comment on either Stowe or *Uncle Tom's Cabin* appeared, as far as I can tell, in any Russian journal until May 1856, although there are numerous occasions when it might well have been mentioned.[7] George Sand, then an international celebrity, got a great deal of journalistic attention during this time (the liberal Petersburg journal *The Contemporary* ran a series on her life), yet we look in vain for any allusion to her role as one of the great early promoters of Stowe's book.[8] Perhaps the most revealing silence occurs in an article in *The Contemporary* in 1854 on the state of American publishing. Nathaniel Hawthorne, James Fenimore Cooper, and Washington Irving are all discussed, along with statistics on readership and sales, but no word about the foremost publishing sensation of the period. Earlier commentators are almost certainly correct in thinking that these absences, in a journalistic atmosphere intensely preoccupied with what was "hot" in the West, point to some wider, unspoken ban.[9]

More direct evidence is provided by an 1858 report on the currently burning topics preoccupying Russia's highest circles of power sent by

Francis Claxton, American consul in Moscow, to Secretary of State Lewis Cass. The novel was in fact just making its way into print in Russia at the time Claxton was finishing up his communiqué (1 January 1858), and the report can be taken to describe the climate of government opinion in the period immediately prior to the publication. The government's intention to abolish serfdom effectively became public knowledge in November 1857, but there was, as Claxton indicates, considerable anxiety that the revelation would provoke uprisings among peasants impatient for change:[10]

> The fear is freely expressed and appears to be generally entertained that serious trouble may arise and blood may be shed; as an indication of this feeling, remonstrances have been made that a translation into Russ [sic] of *Uncle Tom's Cabin* now in press should not be permitted to be published, for as a French translation has for a long time been in the hands of the educated classes, the issue of the one in question is looked upon as purposely incendiary and calculated to mislead the peasantry into the idea that they are no better circumstanced and treated than the slaves in America.[11]

We have to my knowledge no more explicit indication of the tsarist government's attitudes toward *Uncle Tom's Cabin*, although other, broad hints at a prohibition are found in letters and diary entries, some of which I discuss below.[12] Apart from their eyewitness value, Claxton's comments raise the broader question of just how incendiary the novel was felt to be in the 1850s, especially in still-existing slave or serf societies like Brazil, Romania, and Cuba.[13] (Of the US South's attitude, of course, we know considerably more.)[14]

The Russian government, though unduly paranoid about the potential of Stowe's novel to provoke peasant uprisings, was certainly correct in its sense of *Uncle Tom's Cabin*'s notoriety among "the educated classes." Russians living abroad, particularly exiled liberals, apparently read the book as soon as it appeared, most often in translations from French.[15] Already on 8 December 1852, Alexander Herzen (1812–70), foundational figure for the later liberal-radical educated elite and at that time in exile in London, received a letter from his then-friend Vladimir Aristovich Engel'son in Paris: "Have you read *Uncle Tom's Cabin* [title written in English]? I'm reading the feuilletons in the *Presse* and every day I recall our homeland."[16] But Herzen already had his own copy, and two months later (3 February 1853) wrote in turn to his old friend and fellow exile Maria Kasparovna Reikhel': "Have you read

Uncle Tom's Cabin [title written in Russian]? Read it, for God's sake, I'm simply reveling over it (I couldn't manage it in English, though, so I got a [French] translation)."[17]

Stowe's novel made it into Russia as well, of course: Ivan Turgenev (1818–83) read it in 1853, apparently in French, and the diaries of Leo Tolstoy (1828–1910) from the Crimean War period reveal that he bought *Onkel Toms Hütte* on 28 August 1854 and read it through over the next few days.[18] And on 9 September 1854, I. I. Pushchin (1789–1859), in Siberian exile since 1825 for his participation in the Decembrist revolt of that year, informed fellow rebel P. N. Svistunov (1803–89) that "L'Oncle Tom," peregrinating through Siberia, had made it all the way to Irkutsk (on Lake Baikal).[19]

Responses of a more detailed kind are predictably hard to come by, but those we do have find, with Vladimir Engel'son, many points of similarity between the world of *Uncle Tom's Cabin* and that of 1850s Russia. Indeed, in the same letter to Herzen, Engel'son offers a whole series of correspondences: Tom is reminiscent of a Russian Old Believer, Miss Ophelia of a German (and therefore Lutheran) from the Baltic region, and St. Clare is quite simply "an educated Russian landowner of [their] own time."[20]

> Everything about him is Russian: his simple nobility, self-centeredness, elegance, indecisiveness (or laziness), and most of all a lack of all lust for power or money. . . . He's too proud to covet wealth or position, and has too much of a sense of his own worth . . . to be pushy or a scoundrel. . . . And everything in the St. Clare house is Russian: his children love the servants, the servants love the children, and are wasteful and disorderly to boot; the spoiled valet [Adolph] can't distinguish his master's property from his own.[21]

The less appealing Marie St. Clare, in the meantime, is nonetheless a "genuine 'Princess Trubetskaia,' who calls [her husband] a slob and an oaf." The connections extend to literary parallels: Legree recalls the ursine landowner Sobakevich from Gogol's *Dead Souls* (1842), while Cassy, notes Engel'son, is very much like the brutalized peasant actress of Herzen's own antiserfdom tale "The Thieving Magpie" (1848). But when he comes to ask *why* all the similarity, Engel'son can only say that "there aren't many ideas or characters that are unique [to a single place or time]." Other readers, as we shall see, tried to give more elaborate social-historical explanations for what they regarded as "Russian" in Stowe's novel.

On the one hand, the few extant and extended early reactions are largely enthusiastic about Stowe's achievement, with some more critical undertones perceptible as well; on the other, the Russian readers apprehend the novel in quite varied ways, stressing in turn its political effectiveness in the abolitionist cause, its "sentimental power," or its value as a sober and convincing structural analysis of the contradictions of bondage. A strong example of this last emphasis is to be found in a remarkable letter written by yet another Decembrist, Nikolai Ivanovich Turgenev (1789–1871; a distant relative of the novelist). Turgenev, who had been a member of the Imperial Council of State before the events of 1825, published *La Russie et les Russes*, a three-volume account of contemporary Russia with a focus on the serfdom question, in Paris in 1847. The abolitionist Maria Weston Chapman (1806–85), a friend of Stowe, read or heard about Turgenev's work and sent him (she wrote) "certain copies of the *Liberator*, and *Standard*, and *Uncle Tom's Cabin*," to which he responded with a letter in French that Chapman published in the abolitionist gift book *The Liberty Bell* in 1853.[22]

The letter is both a gesture of support from abroad and a reflection on the drastically different possibilities for antislavery activism in Russia and the United States. Momentarily questioning (for rhetorical purposes) the value of a "free press" that enables the expression of "ridiculous" and "odious" proslavery views and concluding that such views effectively refute themselves once aired, Turgenev identifies one especially positive result of America's atmosphere of "free discussion": "Above all, this is no time to doubt the benefits of free discussion, now that we have seen the appearance of that masterpiece of art, of spirit, of sentiment and eloquence, which will bring honor to your nation and to your sex, Madame; *Uncle Tom's Cabin*, that admirable volume, which I read shedding tears, not all of which were of pain and sadness."[23] Later, he goes on to explain the different kinds of "tears" he shed:

> When reading *Uncle Tom's Cabin*, I was more than once sadly struck by the applicability of Mrs. Stowe's accounts to what I know about similar horrors, and not only through reports but through actual cases which passed through my hands [as a member of] the Imperial Council. Many of the scenes described in the book seem like an exact depiction of equally frightful scenes in Russia. When considering the comical aspects of the novel, too, there is not one where I have not recognized some comparable moment in Russian comedies. That delicate lady, the wife of the foolish St. Clare, who regrets that the weakness of her health prevents her from beating her slaves with a [cowhide], reminds me of another lady in

a Russian comedy, who reprimands her chambermaid for the sadness she felt when administering her corporal punishment.[24] The human being is the same everywhere; if you remove from him the restraint of the law, he becomes worse than a ferocious beast.[25]

The "applicability of Mrs. Stowe's accounts" to the faraway Russian situation pertains, on Turgenev's reading as on Engel'son's, not only to the brutal realities of serfdom as such but to more progressive literary treatments of Russian bondage as well: both "actual cases" and "Russian comedies," represented world and mode of representation, harmonize with Stowe's materials and manner. To explain this thoroughgoing similarity, Turgenev, a strong advocate of constitutional monarchy and juridical reform, offers a classic Enlightenment constitutionalist argument, one based on pessimism about human nature and optimism about the law.[26] Only legal limits on landowner caprice (and presumably legal protection of peasant rights as well) can prevent the appearance of barbarities on the estates and deprive the satirists of matter for the stage; and because this is true "everywhere," slaves and planters are indeed serfs and *pomeshchiki* (lords), despite all cultural and geographical distance, and *Uncle Tom's Cabin* a "Russian" book. Thus Turgenev marks the beginning of a line of readers—Chernyshevsky, we will see, is in the same tradition—who read Stowe's novel "analytically," as a book that not only recounts particular "horrors" but also reveals the larger structure (here, an absence of law) that makes the horrors possible.

Something like the opposite emphasis can be found in the more complex response, contained in a letter of 14 March 1855 to Baroness A. D. Bludova, of Alexei Stepanovich Khomyakov (1804–60). Khomyakov is well known as perhaps the greatest of the Slavophile thinkers, a small, informal, but influential group that waged polemical war against the rationalistic "Westernizing" impulse introduced into Russia in the eighteenth century in favor of a conscious return to what was specifically "Russian," particularly (in the Slavophiles' view) the rootedness of the nation in the supposedly harmonious collectivities of the village and the Orthodox Church. With his fellow Slavophiles, Khomyakov denounced the "foulness" of serfdom, although, unlike Nikolai Turgenev, he never freed his own peasants (he owned at least two thousand), contenting himself instead with transferring them from corvée, or day-labor obligations (*barshchina*), to the less onerous "quit-rent" (*obrok*) payments.[27]

Famously erudite and indeed cosmopolitan in his interests, by 1855 Khomyakov had read *Uncle Tom's Cabin* as well. Apparently Baroness

Bludova had mentioned Stowe's novel in a previous letter, but we will need to read Khomyakov's response in light of his broader views on bondage and on Russia itself. For like Turgenev, he could not but read the book as a comment on the "local" situation:

> What shall I say to you about Uncle Tom? They're weeping zealously over him [in Moscow], just like you no doubt wept in St. Petersburg; and just as you do there, here much is found in the book that's familiar to us, although not quite in such a black form as in America—even forty years or so ago, when members of families were sold apart from one another, the American forms of bondage were still somewhat worse than ours. . . . Having dispassionately studied our own problem, I understand well the difference between the condition of the serfs and slavery in the strict sense, although of course I in no way approve of the former. The ethical foundation [of serfdom] is different, and it follows that all its manifestations are different as well, despite an apparent similarity in many specific instances, up to and including appalling cruelty or the display of a still more appalling indifference to humanity.[28]

Khomyakov was of the belief that Russian serfdom, in contrast to the more "criminal" sorts of bondage found in Germanic-controlled lands, found its beginning in sheer "ignorance" and as "a crude policing measure generated by the needs of the state."[29] Crucial to his thoughts on emancipation was an insistence both that the peasants be freed *with* land (partially in order to prevent the creation of an English-style proletariat) and that the traditional village community, or mir, with its grounding in communal land tenure, be preserved through all change. It was the mir, which Khomyakov regarded as an organically self-sustaining and self-correcting social body, that gave Russians, serfs and nobles alike, a moral, social, and religious center that (he argued) long predated serfdom as such.[30]

This is the different "ethical foundation" to which he refers here, and which he intends to contrast with the purely profit-driven transport of sub-Saharan Africans to the United States and their enslavement there. Although, of course, the rise of serfdom is intimately connected with the expansion of the Russian state from the sixteenth century onward (and thus never nearly as different from the colonial American situation as Khomyakov would like to think), the Slavophile points nonetheless, through all the idealization, to an important fact.[31] Serfs were enslaved gradually and on their "home turf," with the result that "the role of tradition in limiting the total control of masters over the lives of their bondsmen was greater in Russia than in the United States."[32] Still, "much is familiar" in Stowe's novel, and Khomyakov finds himself in the comparative historian's predicament of trying to understand strikingly similar phenomena across wide historical/cultural differences.

His solution—that the similarities are epiphenomenal merely—is a facile one, contradicted above all by his own fascinated comparison of *Uncle Tom's Cabin* with Russian scenes, a comparison he now extends into an appreciation of a single character: not Tom (who's "perhaps a bit overdone") or Little Eva ("merely a gracious and graceful sister of Paul Dombey"), but (once again) St. Clare:[33]

> He is like all of us in his elegant refinement, his artistic nature, the softness and gentleness of his disposition, his slothful philanthropy, his sybaritic egotism, the weakness of his ethical convictions and un-Christian indifference to the general good, which he skillfully justifies with deft sophisms. In his soul he casts judgment on evil, after all; and what more should he do? He is right before God and before himself.[34]

Russian serfs, bound together by the peasant community, are fundamentally incomparable to other bondsmen, but nobles are equally refined (read: "Europeanized," cosmopolitan) everywhere, and thus Khomyakov can find in St. Clare a satiric (if also lovable) mirror for his own mind and milieu. (Ivan Goncharov's great *Oblomov* was to appear in 1859—had that novel with its dreamy, slothful, serf-owning protagonist existed, Khomyakov might well have alluded to it.)[35] Yet Khomyakov concludes his comment on Stowe with a reflection that moves beyond questions of "comparability" back to the issue of the novel's effect—that "zealous weeping" he mentions at the outset: "I am certain that Mrs. Stowe's novel will give a significant push to the question of black slavery. Social improvement is more dependent upon the heart than people think—more dependent on the heart, perhaps, than on the mind. For this reason, in my view, women are equal to men as great actors in history, although their role is less visible."[36]

Behind the old banal dualism—one that by no means can account for all the critical work that Stowe's novel performs—is, I think, both a quite uncondescending acknowledgment of the book's power and a strong insight into (as we would say today) how that power is gendered.[37] The admission is striking, coming from the famously intellectual Khomyakov, and strains somewhat against the grain of his own argument and comparisons. For if *Uncle Tom's Cabin* affects the "heart" above all, the details of what links or distinguishes slavery and serfdom may not be all that important, and the novel might give "a significant push" to the question of serfdom as well.

Here we should note that Russian readers, long familiar with "literature of feeling" like Richardson's *Clarissa* (1748), Rousseau's *Nouvelle Héloïse* (1761), Goethe's *Sorrows of Young Werther* (1787), the works of Charles Dickens, and native examples like Nikolai Karamzin's 1792 novella *Poor Liza*, were well primed for an encounter with Stowe's sentimental strategies.[38] Indeed, it has been argued that Karamzin's *Liza*—the tale of an impoverished girl who loses her virginity to a young aristocrat, is deserted by him (after he had promised marriage, of course), and drowns herself after discovering his betrothal to a wealthy widow—should be regarded as the progenitor of a major strain within Russian literature, stretching from Pushkin's "Queen of Spades" (1833) to the great novels of Dostoevsky and Tolstoy's *Resurrection* (1899), which promulgates the sentimentalist argument that

> for one who is rich in spirit, performing virtuous actions is a matter of following not some necessity imposed from the outside, but rather his or her own nature. Developed sensibility is capable by itself of distinguishing between good and bad, and thus has no need for normative morality. It would appear, therefore, that awakening the soul's sensibility is enough to dispel all injustice from human and social relations. . . . Consequently, a work of art is evaluated in terms of its power to move, to unthaw and touch the heart.[39]

Stowe would famously make *feeling* a universal ethical yardstick near the end of *Uncle Tom's Cabin*—"There is one thing that every individual can do,—they can see to it that *they feel right*. An atmosphere of sympathetic influence encircles every human being; and the man or woman who *feels* strongly, healthily and justly, on the great interests of humanity, is a constant benefactor to the human race. See, then, to your sympathies in this matter!"—and it is not difficult to see how a narrative built on this principle might find an appreciative audience in a land where sentimentalism had already spread deep and durable roots.[40]

The first significant mention of *Uncle Tom's Cabin* in the domestic Russian press—in a fascinating anonymous article titled "The Internal Parties in the United States" in the (at that time) center-liberal Moscow journal *Russian Messenger* from May 1856—already records the book's political effect as a fact and comes close to identifying it with its popular success:

Besides [demonstrations], the abolitionist uses another, at once more peaceful and noble and more universal method to oppose the barbarism of the crude defenders of bondage. This method is literature: the abolitionists press it into service for the exposure before the whole world of those scandalous injustices about which the fanatics of slavery are unashamed, and in order to protest against them within the circle of civilized peoples. The wounds inflicted by this weapon are perhaps far more tolerable than some others, but they are finally cured only by curing the vice itself, which they serve to oppose. . . . We saw a stunning example of this in the effect wrought by Mrs. Stowe on the entire educated world with her *Uncle Tom*. They read it in America, devoured it greedily all through Europe—if we're not mistaken, it sold an incredible 200,000 copies. In the opinion of many enlightened readers, a disgraceful stain has been left on the American nation, a stain that darkens even its best aspects, those that constitute its pride and adornment, in a most unpleasant way.[41]

The comment's diction stresses the enormous span of *Uncle Tom's Cabin*'s impact (with language like "universal," "the whole world," "the circle of civilized peoples," "entire educated world," "in America [and] all through Europe"), but refrains from offering any theory about why the novel has proven so irresistible to readers—that is, whether it appeals primarily to the heart or to the mind. (The possibility that the novel's popularity might have little to do with antislavery thought *or* sentiment evidently does not occur to the author.) Rather, it is the mode in which the book is written, its very status as *literature*, that makes it such a universal platform for critique and protest, even if that critique, in this instance, leads to a specific indictment of the United States. Literature, here conceptualized in a way that would become important for later educated elites, creates a far wider community of sensibility than other oppositional "methods" can ever do and thus fashions a context in which wholly new, internationalized forces of political pressure can be brought to bear on specific injustices, over the heads of local power.

Of course, this view presumes a certain dialectical interaction of written text and public sphere: the book's appeal is necessarily to an already existent educated populace, which it in turn enlightens in new ways, and which critically incorporates the book into its own discourse. An optimistic picture to be sure—but is *Uncle Tom*'s moral-political effect really directly measurable in terms of its vast popularity? This last question seems to have prompted Alexander Herzen to produce his longest comment on the novel, contained in the well-known essay "Russian Serfdom." Dated 20 December 1852 and written in French

(but first published in English in three parts in November 1853 in the
London *Leader*), the article presents Herzen's condensed history of serfdom, much fiery polemic against Russian rulers from Ivan III to the
present, and what is probably the earliest published response to *Uncle
Tom's Cabin* by a Russian.

One way to get around the censors was to publish abroad, of course;
Herzen was to have a great career in this kind of publishing, and here
he uses a relatively early opportunity both to rain fire on the Russian
government and subtly to chastise Europeans for their apparent indifference to conditions in Russia. Significantly, his argument is framed,
beginning and end, with provocative references to *Uncle Tom's Cabin*,[42]
which (as his letter to Reikhel' indicates) he was reading even while
writing the "Serfdom" article:

> At the moment when all England was displaying a profound and active
> sympathy for the slaves in the southern states of North America, incited
> thereto by the great work of Mrs. Beecher Stowe, no one seemed to
> remember that nearer to England, across the Baltic, is an entire population
> the legal property of a batch of seigneurs; a population not of 3,000,000
> but of 20,000,000![43]

Stowe's novel is "great," Herzen acknowledges, but he questions
whether the "sympathy" it incites manages to radiate beyond a specific
perimeter, or whether the novel's very strength as a weapon in the US
abolitionist cause does not also generate a certain forgetfulness. This
argument takes a different turn at the end of his article when, after outlining the enormities of serfdom, he writes:

> Surely from time to time it is well that a free voice should be lifted up to
> denounce these degrading institutions, this foul complicity of a govern-
> ment that talks of its strength, with a noblesse that boasts of its enlighten-
> ment. The mask must be torn from these slaveholders of the North [i.e.,
> Russian serf-owners], who go lounging and lisping over Europe, mingling
> with your affairs, assuming the rank of civilized beings,—nay, of liberal-
> minded men, who read *Uncle Tom's Cabin* with horror, and shudder when
> they read of sellers of *black flesh*. Why, these same brilliant spies of the
> *salons* are the very men who on their return to their domains rob, flay, sell
> the *white* slave, and are served at table by their living *property*.[44]

Having already become an antislavery ensign, *Uncle Tom's Cabin* (or the
reading of it) can be used as sentimental wrapping, as another moral
"mask" behind which the "slaveholders of the North" can conceal their
iniquities even from themselves. (We might also wonder whether

Herzen, living in England, could have sensed the way that British enthusiasm for Stowe's attack on US slavery sometimes drifted into "gloating at America's expense"—a sentiment perhaps detectable also in the *Russian Messenger*'s emphasis on the "disgraceful stain . . . left on the American nation"—in a dynamic, which we will encounter more starkly later, energized as much by feelings of national pride and rivalry as by abolitionist commitment.)[45] These two types of reading—the kind that neglects the larger reality of bondage, and the kind that substitutes "sympathy" for (self-)critical analysis of institutions—work together; Herzen sees both as betrayals of the novel's radical promise.

In this respect his comments, though clearly laudatory, presage later suspicions about making easy correlations between the book's moral power and its affective impact. An early example can be found in a harrowing piece by one "P.E." called "Landowners and Peasants" from an 1859 issue of the *Russian Messenger*. After a series of terrible descriptions of starvation and misery in the Vitebsk area (scenes he compares with what he has read of similar horrors in Ireland) the author writes:

> We are used to seeing our serfs as tools, as laboring machines. We demand that these laboring machines be useful to us, and worry very little about the conditions or means through which this result is achieved. Indeed, we are used to their poverty, we are used to attributing it to sloth and negligence, and many of us, endowed with very good souls, are more likely to help an occasional petitioner than to get bothered about the daily needs of our peasants. How many women have I seen weeping inconsolably over *Uncle Tom's Cabin*, but who are never struck by the real misery and poverty so often encountered in our villages. Yet it's not only in America that one finds Uncle Toms.[46]

"Landowners and Peasants" has a confessional aspect, inasmuch as "P.E." is writing as a nobleman deeply frustrated with the course of reform in Russia and thus with his own milieu. But he is also writing, like Herzen, as one of the international "liberal-minded"; he hopes precisely to perform one of those broader comparative "applications" that, Herzen implies, Stowe's book deserves. Thus the comments of both Herzen and "P.E." are true critical interventions, not straightforward celebrations of the "power of literature."

I should reaffirm, at this point, that many readers worldwide, both in the 1850s and later—indeed, into our own time—have shared the muted discomfort with *Uncle Tom* felt by Herzen and "P.E." Does the sentiment mobilized by Stowe's novel, powerful as it is, have any necessary political function or destination? Does the proliferation of commercialized and sensational reworkings of the novel, especially for the stage—and Herzen in London in 1852 might well have known of that city's burgeoning "Tom" showbiz—not demonstrate the ease with which feeling can be tamed and marketed?[47] What of the temporality and efficacy of literary sentiment: is it (or should it be) a fleeting and limited "aesthetic experience," or something more resilient, externalized, and motivating over the long term? More ominously, might fellow feeling *as such* not obscure other, more structural and hard-to-overcome divisions separating white and black, enslaved and free, peasant and nonpeasant, and so on? We might speculate that *Uncle Tom's* early readers in Russia posed these questions about sentiment and separation with even greater urgency than elsewhere, given their own cosmopolitan investment in the moral efficacy of literary discourse and their historical location in a serf society far distant geographically and distinct socially from the US South. At any rate, their preoccupations, however inchoately expressed in the early 1850s, have been shared by the most probing Anglo-American critics of Stowe's novel right to the present day.[48]

A possible next or alternative step would be to actually appropriate Stowe's model with an eye to more direct application to the Russian problem, and indeed Herzen's article contains a disguised reference to just such a project. He mentions at the beginning that "a friend of [his] proposed to publish a pamphlet to remind English charity of [the fact of serfdom]," but that "his pamphlet was never published."[49] It seems certain that the "friend" was fellow émigré Ivan Gavrilovich Golovin (b. 1816), peripatetic hack author of works on political economy, sketches of Russian life, memoirs, a volume of "American impressions" called *Stars and Stripes* (1856), and what seems to have been a novel-length imitation of Stowe about a "Russian Tom," in French.[50] Apparently the manuscript was purchased by one Nelson from Edinburgh (Golovin, like Herzen, spent some time in England) but was never published.[51]

Alas, as it turns out, we do not know of any full-scale transpositions of *Uncle Tom's Cabin* into the serf context (although some later adaptations certainly add Russifying touches, as we shall see). What is really fascinating, however, is that Golovin seems to have recycled his reading of Stowe's novel for a slightly later work on slavery: a three-act play called *Rovira*, devoted to "the life of slaves in Cuba," and published in Russian in Leipzig in 1858. Dedicated to Alexander von Humboldt (with whose "book in hand," Golovin claims, he traveled through Cuba), *Rovira* tells the story of the handsome mulatto Rodrigo Rovira, owner-operator of a coffeehouse in Havana and beloved of the wealthy Antoinetta Lorenzo.[52] Antoinetta's racist father is opposed to their union, and upon discovering that the Rovira family is descended from slaves, exposes their origins and attempts to return them to bondage. His plans are foiled, however, and at the end he is reconciled with both daughter and (now) son-in-law.

It turns out that Rodrigo Rovira is also an inventor—shades of George Harris—and the play finds a happy resolution in part because of his sale of his main invention, a machine for extracting sugar with steam, to a slave trader from Georgia (United States) named Brown. (The sale turns out to have ambiguously beneficial modernizing effects on the slavery front as well, for as Brown puts it, "one machine like that" can replace "a thousand loads of Negroes.") It is the personage of the American Brown, however, that suggests Golovin's debt to *Uncle Tom's Cabin* most strongly, for this character seems to be an amalgam of all of Stowe's nasty slave trader types, with aspects of Haley, Tom Loker, and even Simon Legree perceptible in the representation. Here is his first entrance (act 2, scene 1):

[*An American with a beard, chewing tobacco, dressed in nankeen, knocks on the door and enters.*]

BROWN: Señor Rovira?
ROVIRA: At your service.
BROWN [*sits down, puts both feet up on the table, and spits on the floor*]:
I've got some business to discuss with you. I'm Mr. Brown from Georgia—traveling around doing some trading.
ROVIRA: What's your business, exactly?
BROWN: Why hide the truth? I'm involved in the black slave trade.
[*Rovira pushes away a chair in disgust.*] A few days ago we brought in a cargo of blacks, dressed up like sailors—if things turn out, we'll take some of them to New Orleans.[53]

Like Stowe's ruffians, Brown also makes a point of consuming alcohol and chooses to down some rum instead of a draught of "pineapple syrup with water" offered him by Rovira. *Othello*, it is not—but Golovin's play does strongly suggest that the issue of slavery world-wide was coming to be imagined through the tropes and types of *Uncle Tom's Cabin*. For while Brown comes from Georgia, and the play itself is set in Cuba, Golovin's dedication to Humboldt and Humboldt's response (both published in French as a frontispiece to the play itself) touch less on Cuban slavery and more on the question of Russian bondage and

Russian involvement in slavery-related issues. Golovin praises Alexander II as the monarch for whom "the glory of emancipating the serfs" is reserved, and Humboldt writes both of his own friendship with Wilberforce and of how he admired Alexander I's strong opposition to the slave trade as expressed at the Third Congress of Aix-la-Chapelle (1818).[54] Thus what is at least in part a rewriting of Stowe (and specifically the George and Eliza plot) becomes an occasion for a kind of quilting together of different contexts of bondage and abolition, a rough attempt at "totalization," if you will.

It is clear then that *Uncle Tom's Cabin* had at least a considerable reputation if not indeed a wide readership in Russia prior to its first domestic publication at the end of 1857–beginning of 1858. A review of Stowe's *Dred* that appeared in *The Contemporary* in the first half of 1857 doesn't even mention Stowe's earlier novel, and it is difficult to tell if this omission is due to censorship or whether mentioning *Uncle Tom* would already have seemed superfluous—although the fact that the anonymous reviewer never refers to Dred's fundamental role as leader of a slave revolt does imply that caution was still being taken.[55]

The publication in November 1857 of the famous imperial rescript, calling upon nobles in the Lithuanian provinces to form committees to work on laws outlining "a systematic amelioration of the way of life [of] the proprietary peasants," was generally taken as a signal that a real, Russia-wide emancipation process had in fact begun.[56] Certainly, the announcement marked the beginning of a year or so of relative freedom to publish on the serfdom question, and it is within that privileged span of time that three different Russian editions of *Uncle Tom's Cabin* appeared: from December 1857 through March 1858 in the *Russian Messenger*, in 1858 (individual chapters only) in *Son of the Fatherland*, and all at once in January 1858 as a supplement to the *Contemporary*.

On 25 December 1857, Nikolai Nekrasov (1821–78), major poet and coeditor (with Ivan Panaev) of the *Contemporary*, wrote to Ivan Turgenev in Rome about the state of the journal and upcoming plans:

> Regarding the journal, I shall tell you that its serious section is not bad, but things are in a bad way when it comes to stories! They do not exist. . . . [As a consequence] subscriptions began to fall; to increase them we have thought up a "Historical Library." This was followed by an opportunity to translate *Uncle Tom's Cabin*. I have decided to incur an unforeseen expenditure: the novel is to be offered gratis with issue no. 1, this announcement leading to a jump in subscriptions. It is noteworthy that

this has been most opportune: the question is very much in the public eye in respect to our own Negroes.[57]

Nekrasov's note, brief as it is, is worthy of attention and unpacking. First of all, it provides a clear indication that Stowe's novel had indeed rather suddenly become "publishable," and certainly some of the "unforeseen expenditure" went toward work on the translation itself, which (like the *Messenger* version, most likely) was done at great speed. The journal's expense sheet for honoraria indicates that six translators were employed; intriguingly enough, a man named Pavel Mikhailovich Novosil'skij (1802-62) was not only involved in the translation of both the *Messenger* and the *Contemporary* editions, but was also the government censor who gave the *Contemporary* permission to publish *Uncle Tom's Cabin* in the first place.[58] Out of 731 rubles paid to the translators working for the *Contemporary*, 500 went to Novosil'skij—who translated (according to the same record of honoraria) a mere 7 pages out of 476! Plainly enough, part of the "unforeseen expenditure" included a token of appreciation for the censor, who no doubt sped the text's passage through the committee.[59]

The note also offers insight into what we might call the book's dual instrumentality. On the one hand, the subject of *Uncle Tom's Cabin* is obviously politically timely in relation to the peasant question; on the other, the novel proves to be a popular hit even prior to publication, "leading to a jump in subscriptions." (We shouldn't miss the hint Nekrasov drops to Turgenev to send some stories along, either.) The dichotomy is a telling one, and we will encounter repetitions of it later, when we will see "edifying" models for literacy attempting to make their way through a growing mass market of readers.

What was immediately important for Nekrasov, however, was that the Russian translation attracted readers straightaway, and indeed many of those who had already read the novel in some other language picked up one or another Russian version as soon as they appeared. I. I. Pushchin, now returned from exile, wrote to his wife on 14 February 1858 that he was going through the *Contemporary* translation, predicting that some of the serf holders around Moscow wouldn't be able to wait for the *Russian Messenger* installments and would have to send to Petersburg for the full version.[60]

Pushchin adds, however, that the *Messenger* version is a superior translation; and although he doesn't go into details, his observation is undoubtedly correct, particularly in terms of actual completeness. Apparently, all Russian translations prior to 1883 were based on French or German versions, thus compelling any student of those early Russian versions to examine them through the non-English intermediaries.[61] Notwithstanding Novosil'skij's "involvement" in both versions, the two translations seem to derive from different French editions, with the *Contemporary* version more marked by the censor's pen. But which censor, the French or the Russian? As so often with censorship, inconsistencies and inexplicable choices abound.

If one is searching for sections of Stowe's novel that might have proven sore points for the pre-emancipation Russian censorship, the chapters "Miss Ophelia's Experiences, Continued," "Henrique," and "Reunion"—with their references to European bondage and class unrest worldwide—would seem the perfect places to begin. St. Clare's famous prediction of a *"dies irae,"* for example, from "Miss Ophelia's Experiences, Continued":

> One thing is certain,—that there is a mustering among the masses, the world over; and there is a *dies irae* coming on, sooner or later. The same thing is working in Europe, in England, and in this country. My mother used to tell me of a millennium that was coming, when Christ should reign, and all men should be free and happy. (Stowe, 240)

As it turns out, the *Russian Messenger* translation cuts perhaps the most inflammatory sentence ("The same thing is working in Europe . . .")—but leaves virtually all other references to class inequality in the novel intact, including this exchange between St. Clare and Miss Ophelia in "Reunion," perhaps the touchiest one of all from an east-of-the-Elbe point of view:

> "Do you suppose it possible that a nation ever will voluntarily emancipate?" said Miss Ophelia.
> "I don't know," said St. Clare. "This is a day of great deeds. Heroism and disinterestedness are rising up, here and there, in the earth. The Hungarian nobles set free millions of serfs, at an immense pecuniary loss; and, perhaps, among us may be found generous spirits, who do not estimate honor and justice by dollars and cents." (Stowe, 322)[62]

By contrast, the *Contemporary* version leaves the *"dies irae"* prediction untouched, while cutting or altering several passages touching on comparable subject matter. Sometimes the cuts are predictable, such as the omission in the "Henrique" chapter of all the unnerving talk between

St. Clare and Alfred of Louis XVI, the French noblesse, sansculottes, "contemptible Hayti," and the now dangerously dispersed superiority of Anglo-Saxon blood.[63] Other changes demand more complex evaluation, as in this version of the "Hungarian nobles" passage:

> "Do you really think that a country could agree to emancipate all of its Negroes at once?"
>
> "I don't know. But we live in an age of great events. Heroism and disinterestedness are beginning to raise their voices across the globe. Perhaps in America will be found great-spirited people, who do not measure honor and truth by the same standard as cotton and sugar."[64]

At first glance, the distortion seems quite obvious and readable: besides the simple omission of the Hungarian nobles, the decisions to replace "voluntarily emancipate" with "emancipate all of its Negroes," "among us" with "in America," and (most brilliantly) "dollars and cents" with "cotton and sugar," have the effect of subtly "Americanizing" an exchange that in Stowe has a distinctly global field of reference. In fact, however, except for that rude purging of the Hungarian nobles, the entire section is a direct translation from the French "original," and not an example of censorial cunning.[65] The effect remains the same, of course, but is largely due to a hidden, unexpected mediation.

The question of why the *French* translation contains these changes is a vexing one that I have yet to solve. In her excellent study of *Uncle Tom* in France, Edith Lucas discusses the various early translations primarily in terms of style and general fidelity, rather than censorship and ideology. However, she does mention that *Uncle Tom* appeared in the immediate wake of the crushing of the revolts of 1848, following which (especially after 1851) harsh censorship of political discourse was reintroduced, which might explain the convenient "Americanization."[66]

Other changes, at any rate, are likely unique to the Russian version in the *Contemporary*. We sometimes find rather straightforward substitutions used to inflect Stowe's critique back toward the US South when it strains toward a more universal application. A good example is the following section from the debate in the "Henrique" chapter:

"For my part, I think half this republican talk sheer humbug. It is the educated, the intelligent, the wealthy, the refined, who ought to have equal rights and not the canaille."	"For my part, I regard half of these republican phrases as a kind of bad joke. Educated, rich, and enlightened people require equal rights, but not *Negroes*," [said Alfred.]
Cont. p. 30	*Cont. p. 30*

"If you can keep the canaille of that opinion," said Augustine. "They took *their* turn once, in France."

"Of course, they must be kept down, consistently, steadily, as I should," said Alfred, setting his foot hard down, as if he were standing on somebody.

"It makes a terrible slip when they get up," said Augustine,—"in St. Domingo, for instance."

"Poh!" said Alfred, "we'll take care of that, in this country. We must set our face against all this educating, elevating talk, that is getting about now; the lower class must not be educated." (Stowe, 276)

"If you can make *Negroes* partake of that opinion," answered Augustine.

"Of course, one has to curb *Negroes* with consistency and firmness, just as I would do," said Alfred, trampling the ground with his foot, as though it were one of his enemies.

"*Negroes* wreak terrible devastation when they take it into their heads to rebel—as in San Domingo, for example."

"Oh, we'll avoid all of that here. We simply have to place obstacles in the way of this desire to educate, which is spreading these days. *Negroes* must not be educated."[67] (*Contemporary* translation, p. 288, italics mine)

Obviously enough, the substitution of "Negroes" for "canaille" is made easier by St. Clare's reference to San Domingo, but this change requires in its turn that St. Clare's reminder of the canaille having taken "*their* turn once, in France" be eliminated. The alteration, crude as it is, effectively respatializes Stowe's discourse and converts Alfred from a comprehensive reactionary into a merely (and safely) American racist.

At the same time, much in the book that might be thought "inflammatory" in the tsarist context is retained in the *Contemporary* edition—most notably St. Clare's analysis of the "root and nucleus" of slavery (Stowe, 230–31) and his discussion of the limits of aristocratic sympathy (Stowe, 233) in Chapter 19. (Nor, apparently, did Stowe's "Saxonist" racial ideology raise many eyebrows—an issue to which we will return later.) Inconsistencies like this are hard to explain, especially in detail; probably some combination of haste, negotiation, idiosyncrasy of judgment, and the specificities of the French source produced the somewhat-altered text that Nekrasov finally published. Unclear, too, are the reasons for the heavier censorship of the *Contemporary* version, although perhaps both Nekrasov's rush to publish the whole book (which would have drawn attention in itself) and the journal's more radical reputation led to harsher scrutiny—with the result that the more "conservative" *Russian Messenger* printed a considerably more accurate version. What is important to stress at this point is that the story of the first translations introduces themes that will stretch across the whole history of *Uncle Tom*'s translation and reception in Russia: the ambiguous shaping force of political interest (whether governmental or not) on the text; the way in which changes to the text often involve a revision of the book's social/geopolitical coordinates; and aspirations both to reach out to a wide readership and to boost sales.

After Serfdom, before October

Such children are very common among us, and such men and
women, too. How are they to be governed?
    St. Clare

GAUGING IN DETAIL the immediate response to the Russian translations is difficult. To my knowledge, no reviews appeared,
although we do have a few letters reporting strong reactions (like those
of Leo Tolstoy, discussed below). It is worth noting, however, that
government censors, who sometimes expressed their concerns about a
text after it was already published, voiced some displeasure about the
contents of the December 1857 issue of the *Russian Messenger*. The focus
of their ire was apparently a three-page narrative poem by Prince
G. Kugushev titled "Duniasha," a gothic ballad about a landowner who
cruelly imprisons the young serf woman Duniasha and kills her and
her merchant lover when he discovers them together. However, the
actual memo circulated among the Ministry of Education's censors refers
only to the more general need, in the wake of the imperial rescripts, to
pay "the strictest attention" to articles and poems that might contain
"harsh and biting judgments about the relation of lords and landowners
to servants and peasants," and so may betray some anxiety about *Uncle
Tom's Cabin* as well.[1]

The book (in a reprint of the *Russian Messenger* translation) was still
on sale in 1860, but apart from an early and remarkable adapted version
from 1862 (discussed below), I have been unable to identify any editions
published between 1858 and 1871, and only one between 1871–1880,
after which point the publication history is fairly continuous until

32

around 1930. The proclamation of 1861 was met by considerable agitation among peasants skeptical about the terms of the emancipation
(which involved the continuation of services to the gentry as part of the
redemption arrangement) and a couple of major uprisings.[2] The result
on the journalistic level was a noticeable toughening of the censorship,
which may have deemed a reappearance of Stowe's novel undesirable.

In any event, the novel had already become a part of the mental world
of the educated elites, with strongly positive and negative attitudes
clearly formed by the early 1860s. Thus Nikolai Chernyshevsky (1828–
89), the great journalist, political thinker, and later martyred hero for
Russian radicals, echoed Nikolai Turgenev's praise of Stowe's powers
of social analysis in an 1858 response to an article by one "Mr. Provincial" in the *Contemporary*. "Mr. Provincial" is at pains to show, against
authors who would present landowners as evil sadists, that they are in
fact sensitive people concerned about the plight of their peasants. In a
remarkably modern-sounding argument, Chernyshevsky uses Stowe
to demonstrate that what matters in situations of exploitation is not the
individual disposition of the landlord but rather what we would call
the "structural positions" of lord and bondsman:

> Neither in Europe nor Asia do we find anything as offensive to the sense
> of justice as slavery in the southern United States. . . . Yet nonetheless,
> look more closely at the main idea even of Stowe's novel: does she really
> look at the planters with animosity, does she really wish evil and loss
> upon them? No, she presents the greater number of the planters in her
> story as people who in their personalities earn the respect of many of
> those around them, as highly worthy people.[3] However, these people
> own Negroes—moreover, they raise their voices for the preservation of
> slavery. They are simply wrong in their reckonings, or take pleasure in
> the routine associated with that way of life. Although they are, in terms
> of their position, people harmful to the nation, they remain in large part
> respectable people, personally considered.[4]

By contrast, Dmitri Pisarev (1840–68), successor to Chernyshevsky
after 1862 as the leading radical (or "Nihilist") critic, offered an equally
compelling but diametrically opposed judgment of Stowe's novel,
arguing that the book's reliance on convention and "idealization" bars
the path to any genuine engagement with social reality:

> If we want to be disinterested, . . . we will have to recognize that the ideal-
> ization evident in the way the characters and conditions of the Negroes
> are drawn [in *Uncle Tom's Cabin*] seriously damages not only the artistic

wholeness of the representation but the persuasiveness of the conclusions drawn. By compromising the poetic truth of her creation in the name of her social goal, Stowe fails even to achieve that prime objective fully.[5]

Pisarev was one of the most intriguing and paradoxical early European theorists of "autonomy" of both creative practice and reader response; a true dialectician, his defense of autonomy was always (and especially in his last works) mounted in the name of broader social goals, with an eye to producing independent subjectivities capable of building and sustaining a free community.[6] At the early stage during which the comment on Stowe's novel was written (1860–61), Pisarev's interest in independence took the form of a negativity vis-à-vis existing order, and an emphasis on the need "to emancipate the person from all the trammels imposed on him by the timidity of his own thoughts, by caste prejudices, the authority of tradition, by any striving toward a common ideal, and all the antiquated rubbish that prevents a living man from breathing freely and developing in every direction."[7] This statement, I think, provides a crucial clue for understanding Pisarev's denunciation of Stowe's "idealization," one that interestingly presages James Baldwin's much later (1949) critique. *Uncle Tom's Cabin*, he implies, is not only patently manipulative; it mobilizes old, conventional, religious machinery *in order to* manipulate, and the obviousness and pushiness of this strategy stands at odds, for a sensitive reader, with the book's larger emancipatory message.

Thus even within the radical camp, the dual conception of the novel as at once realistic description of slavery and effective "engaged" literature proved an unstable one. Is the book's analysis of bondage accurate even if its reliance on stereotype and cliché is manifest? Can the book be effective even if it isn't "realistic" (or truthful)? Or do its shortcomings as a "realist" work of art compromise its political validity as well? We can track the vicissitudes of these doubts by looking at the contrasting responses to the novel by two major writers, Ivan Turgenev and Leo Tolstoy, who have been more closely linked (in an anecdotal way) to *Uncle Tom's Cabin* than any other Russian authors. As we shall see, their assessments of the novel over time went in distinctly different directions.

It has become something of a commonplace to compare *Uncle Tom's Cabin* with some of the early work of Turgenev, in particular of course those works that describe critically the world of serfs and masters, such as *Sketches from a Hunter's Notebook* (published 1852) and the stories

"Mumu" (1852) and "The Inn" ("Postoialyj dvor," written 1852, published 1855). It seems that the tradition of comparing Stowe and Turgenev began in France in 1854, when Ernest Charrière, the first French translator of the *Sketches*, made the juxtaposition in his introductory article.[8] Later in the same year, a series of selections from Turgenev's book appeared in English (translated from French) as "Photographs from Russian Life" in the London journal *Fraser's Magazine for Town and Country*.[9] After acknowledging "that we know as little of the interior life of Russia as of that of Dahomey or Timbuctoo," the anonymous prefacer suggests that Turgenev's "Photographs" offer the kind of "uncoercive" critique of bondage that writers like Pisarev claimed was wanting in Stowe:[10]

> M. Ivan [Turgenev's] "photographs" are the more interesting, inasmuch as he is not a professed writer; he has not sought "effects," but has transferred to paper, with the vividness of a daguerreotype, the impressions produced upon him by the various personages and scenes he describes. . . . If there are those who seek the artificial stimulus of horrors, who like to hear with the mind's ear the fall of the knout on the back of the suffering serf, or who desire that the simpler pictures of slave life shall be set in a connected narrative of refined cruelty and pain, as in the work of Mrs. Stowe, they will not find their appetite satisfied in the passage we propose to give. . . . [Turgenev] moralizes not in words but in examples. He does not spare his own class, but he lets the facts speak for themselves; and as his sufferers are not angels but Russians habituated to serfdom and its evils, you are able to look at that institution somewhat more philosophically than if your moral indignation were perpetually excited by artificial means. The bright side is given, as well as the dark one, and yet the result of the whole is a profound conviction of the iniquity of serfdom as an institution, and of its degrading effects on the subject as well as on the master. The book is a Russian *Uncle Tom's Cabin*, without its blood and gunpowder.[11]

Thus began a certain tradition of regarding the *Sketches* as an "artistically superior" antibondage book, a tradition whose most famous exponent is surely Henry James.[12] That Stowe was not fundamentally attempting with *Uncle Tom* to produce a "work of art," and that suggesting that she was commits, in Lawrence Buell's words, "the anachronism of imputing *novelistic* intent [to Stowe]," probably could not have been noticed by many writers at the time, implicated as they were in the emergence of the vocation of the novelist as such.[13] Stowe later did write "novels," of course, and part of the complexity of the reception of *Uncle Tom* worldwide lies in the way the book commingles and confounds political-evangelical with artistic ambition: a writer might exert enormous effects with a book, but perhaps only if he or she refrains from writing a "novel."

All the same, the first Russian to make the Stowe/Turgenev comparison—as usual, Alexander Herzen—stresses less the restraint and "realism" of Turgenev than his "sentimental power." In an article "On the Rural Novel in Russia," written just as *Uncle Tom's Cabin* was first appearing in the *Russian Messenger* (28 December 1857), Herzen praises the moral intensity of the *Sketches*, calling them a "martyrology for the peasant."[14] Adding a reference to the suffering hero of the harrowing story "Mumu" (about a domestic serf whose isolation drives him to drink), Herzen presents Turgenev as the same sort of encyclopedist of Russian bondage as Stowe is of American:

> Turgenev did not stop with [his] martyrology for the peasant; without fear he also went to find the household serf inside his stifling chamber, where the only consolation is alcohol. He has tracked down for us the existence of these Russian Uncle Toms, with his capacity as artist, defying both a double censorship by the government and at the same time making us tremble at accounts of this base, inhuman suffering, to which one generation after another succumbs, without hope and not only with an outraged soul, but with a body covered in wounds.[15]

Although suggestions that the *Sketches* played a polemical role in Russia comparable to that of *Uncle Tom's Cabin* in the United States are plainly exaggerated, it seems that the juxtaposition of the works became a trope for educated elites in several countries quite early, and later Russian prefaces to Stowe's novel regularly make the comparison.[16]

The situation is more complex in regard to Turgenev's own response to Stowe. In spite of the fact that he fathered a daughter with one of his bondswomen—not uncommon in Russia, though less prevalent than in the US South—of Turgenev's fundamental hostility to the institution of serfdom there can be no question, and reading the *Sketches* and other works written between 1847 and 1855 as in part "tendentious" is certainly not wrong.[17] As already mentioned, he first read *Uncle Tom's Cabin* in 1853; at the time he was in exile on his estate of Spasskoye, supposedly for having written a commemoration of Gogol but more probably because of the *Sketches*. Later he met Stowe in Paris during her second trip to Europe in 1856, and she and her daughters made a sufficient impression for Turgenev to mention them in a letter of 5 December 1856 to A. Druzhinin. He described Stowe as "a kind, simple, and just imagine! shy American woman; with her were two red-haired daughters in red burnouses with wild crinolines—very odd figures."[18] This appreciation of the "New England exotic" was probably the first Russian representation of Stowe-the-person, who would later become important in her own right as (among other things) an inspirational myth of the "simple" woman who, through diligence and imagination, achieved great things with her pen.

For clues to the Russian author's deeper response to *Uncle Tom's Cabin*, we have to look at a couple of moments in two other Turgenev works, the story "The Inn" and the later novel *Smoke* (1867). "The Inn," written in exile in 1852, tells the tragic story of an earthy, life-loving serf peasant named Akim. Akim is an entrepreneurial spirit who builds an inn and marries an attractive younger peasant woman; he has the misfortune of having both inn and wife taken away from him through both the machinations of a young conman and seducer named Naum and the stupidity and indifference of his owner. After contemplating revenge, he eventually blames himself for the folly of having "wanted to live with a young wife for [his] own pleasure" and becomes a wandering pilgrim.[19]

Turgenev was apparently satisfied with the story at first and wrote to one of his correspondents, "I've gone straighter to the mark [than in the *Sketches*] because at the time of writing it I'm not thinking about publication."[20] But he seems to have changed his mind in response to criticisms leveled by his friend Pavel Vasilievich Annenkov (1812–87), a literary critic and member of the liberal Belinsky circle, most famous for editing the first collected edition of Pushkin's works (1850–60). Annenkov read "The Inn" prior to its publication in 1855 and had at first praised the work, noting only a few technical inaccuracies in Turgenev's representation of serf-owner relations. But a letter of 12 April 1853 finds much more to criticize in the story, in particular its subjection of art to "polemic," a reproach that Annenkov reinforces with a comparison: "See now what another Akim, Uncle Tom, is doing now throughout the world with his cabin. Yet in all probability, not one extra gray hair will be added to our already gray heads when Uncle Tom ends up being forgotten. That's not to say that the whole thing's not very noble, filled with warmth, and there are superlative pages here. But Uncle Tom and Uncle Akim are polemic, not creation."[21] Turgenev's reply of a few days later not only indicates his acceptance of Annenkov's observation, but his response to Stowe's novel and a new artistic resolve as well: "As far as *Uncle Tom* goes, which I read through over the last few days, I was struck by the notion myself, that after all

Akim is really of that same caliber. Your letter strengthened that impression, as a consequence of which I promised myself never to write this sort of thing again."[22]

It is obvious enough that Turgenev has no high estimate of *Uncle Tom*'s "caliber." In truth, the exchange between author and critic is a peculiar one, because the pious, unworldly Uncle Tom hardly resembles the sensuous, practical (if gullible) Akim at all. Only in their mutual eschewing of violence, and of course in the tragedy of their stories, are they alike—although Annenkov oddly seems to read Tom's tragedy as essentially the loss of his *property*, which suggests a subtle "Russianizing" of his perception of American bondage as presented by Stowe. In any event, we can see here how the very mention of *Uncle Tom's Cabin* is already becoming a telegraphic watchword for "tendentious" literature as such, whether evaluated positively or negatively.

Stowe and her novel resurface rather bizarrely later in Turgenev's oeuvre near the beginning of his satirical novel *Smoke*. Four years after meeting Stowe (on 23 October 1860), Turgenev reported to Herzen that some strange rumors were circulating about him among the Russian exiles in Heidelberg, Germany, where he was living at the time: "Evidently, the city of Heidelberg excels in the fabrication of gossip. . . . People are saying that I'm holding a serf mistress against her will, and that mistress Beecher Stowe (!) publicly reproached me for this, and that I swore at her."[23] No biography of either Turgenev or Stowe mentions this incident, so I think we can assume that "fabrication" it was. In *Smoke*, however, Turgenev recycles the story as part of his mockery of the mean-spirited "radical" pretensions of the émigré world, a satire he fashioned in response to the hostile reaction among radicals to *Fathers and Sons* (1862). The novel is set in Baden-Baden, and much of it is taken up with ludicrously heated debates among the Russians there: essentially, a stew of political discussion, gossip, and character assassination. During one of these colloquies in the fourth chapter, Madame Sukhantchikoff (who is a caricature of liberal feminists of the 1860s) attacks a certain Tenteleeff (not present at the gathering) for his hypocrisy and former cruelty toward his serfs:

> "As every one knows, he was the most dreadful tyrant with his people, although he gave himself out as an emancipator. Well, one day he was sitting with some acquaintances in Paris, when, all of a sudden, in comes Mrs. Beecher Stowe,—well, you know, 'Uncle Tom's Cabin.' Tenteleeff, a frightfully conceited man, began to urge the host to present him; but as soon as Mrs. Stowe heard his name: 'What?'—says she:—

'how dares he make acquaintance with the author of "Uncle Tom"?' And, whack, she slapped his face!—'Begone!' says she,—'this instant!'—And what do you think? Tenteleeff took his hat, and putting his tail between his legs, he slunk off."

"Well, that strikes me as exaggerated," remarked Bambaeff.—"That she did say 'Begone!' to him is a fact; but she did not slap his face."

"She did slap his face, she did slap his face," repeated Madame Sukhantchikoff, with convulsive intensity:—"I don't talk nonsense. And you are the friend of such people!"[24]

Besides settling a few scores with people now long forgotten, Turgenev is associating Stowe and her work with a certain self-righteous, hysterical stance of "protest" that he felt was characteristic of the radical crowd; on his version, rather than appealing to good sense and tolerance, Stowe's novel and legend are readily converted into vehicles for faux-political outcries by the sentimental and the shallow.

Such a judgment presages that strain of Stowe reception that stresses not only her work's lack of "artistry"—a reproach found in the earliest Russian responses to *Uncle Tom*—but also what are felt to be traces of puritanical narrowness,[25] as in this entry on "Beecher Stowe" from the 1891 edition of the famous Brockhaus-Efron encyclopedia:

> Her novel *Uncle Tom's Cabin* (1852) appeared on the scene as a kind of new revelation. In spite of its artistic weakness, it sold 350,000 copies in the first year in America, and 600,000 copies overall. . . . Her other works lag far behind this novel even from an artistic perspective, [and her exposure of Byron in "Lady Byron Vindicated"] can be explained only with reference to the puritanical intolerance of the social environment in which Stowe lived from the time of her marriage.[26]

We see this skeptical attitude reemerging, in a rather different key, during the early Soviet period as well, when Stowe's "puritan protest" met with some especially harsh assessments.[27]

In the meantime, however, what we might call the dominant reception of *Uncle Tom's Cabin* in late nineteenth-century Russia is quite precisely celebratory of Stowe, her moral power, and her religious grounding. Nowhere more so than in Tolstoy's appreciation in *What Is Art?* (1897), in what is probably the best-known comment on Stowe by any Russian author:

> The Christian art of our time can be, and actually is, of two sorts: (1) the art which conveys sentiments which arise from the religious consciousness

of man's position in the world, in relation to God and to our neighbor,—religious art, and (2) the art which conveys the simplest sensations of life, such as are accessible to all men of the whole world,—vital, national, universal art. It is only these two kinds of art that in our time may be regarded as good art. . . . If I were required to point out in modern art the models of each of these kinds of art, I should point, as to models of a higher art, which arises from the love of God and of our neighbor, in the sphere of literature, to Schiller's *Robbers*; from the moderns, to Hugo's *Les Pauvres Gens* and to his *Les Misérables*; to Dickens's stories and novels, *Tale of Two Cities*, *Chimes*, and others, to *Uncle Tom's Cabin*, to Dostoevsky, especially his *Dead House*, to George Eliot's *Adam Bede*.[28]

It would certainly be worthwhile, though far beyond the scope of this essay, to determine the affinities of Stowe's work to all these disparate "high literary" products from a Tolstoyan perspective. Surely, Tolstoy's judgment here is partially responsible for lifting *Uncle Tom's Cabin* to the empyrean of the Euro-American canon, from which it has never been entirely excluded (but to which it has never comfortably belonged, either).[29] This is ironic, of course, and not only because of Tolstoy's own negative late attitude toward that canon in general. Tolstoy's aesthetics in *What Is Art?* plainly belong in the great Russian sentimentalist tradition discussed earlier:

> The religious perception of our times does not select any one society of men; on the contrary it demands the union of all—absolutely of all people without exception. . . . And therefore the feelings transmitted by the art of our time not only cannot coincide with the feelings transmitted by former art [confined as they were to particular segments of society], but must run counter to them.[30]

It can nonetheless be argued that the effect of *Uncle Tom's Cabin*, and perhaps some of the intent behind it, worked to divide as much as to unify. But Stowe's novel can disarm even a reader as confident as Tolstoy; and it turns out that the count came to celebrate *Uncle Tom* only later in life, having apparently dismissed it after his initial reading in 1854.

On 19 February 1858, Nekrasov wrote to Tolstoy asking him how he liked the January issue of the *Contemporary*. With typical forthrightness, the count replied two days later that it was "very bad." Some of the pieces (by authors like Turgenev [*Asya*] and the playwright Alexander Ostrovsky) were below standard; the verses by the great poet (and Tolstoy's friend) Afanasy Fet contained misprints; and besides, Tolstoy complained, "The political pepper strewn all over the journal and in the supplement *Uncle Tom* is not suitable, in my opinion, for the *Contemporary* and will never compare in any event with the pepper contained in the Moscow journals, [especially] under the conditions of the Moscow censorship."[31] As we know, Tolstoy was probably mistaken about the relative severity of the censorships in the two cities, if only in this instance. But his remark seems to betray a strongly negative attitude, at this relatively early period, to tendentious or politically "peppery" material.

The reality is more complex. Tolstoy began but never completed a semiautobiographical novel about serfdom, of which a fascinating fragment remains, titled "A Landlord's Morning" (1852), that explores the morally contradictory position of a young master who (like Tolstoy) wants to improve the lives of his serfs. After the emancipation, he completed the story "Polikushka" (1863), about a good-natured but hard-drinking household serf who commits suicide after losing some money that he was charged with delivering. The underlying antipathy toward serfdom in both of these works is plain, and after unsuccessfully attempting to free his own serfs in 1856 (the peasants were suspicious of the terms of their owner's proposal), Tolstoy served as a peace commissioner of the emancipation settlement in his home province of Tula in 1861.

Nonetheless, that Tolstoy had at least some misgivings about his antiserfdom work is suggested by a couple of exchanges from the 1860s with the above-mentioned Afanasy Fet (1820–92). Fet, one of the major lyric poets of the Russian language, effectively stopped publishing from the midsixties until the early 1880s because of fierce attacks launched by radical critics like Chernyshevsky, Pisarev, and Belinsky against his insistence on the artist's necessary, absolute detachment from social concerns. Fet's aesthetic views were not unconnected to his more general conservatism, however, of which his criticism of "Polikushka" (in a letter to Tolstoy of 11 April 1863) comes as a startling revelation.[32] Arguing from what might be called a neoclassical perspective, Fet insists that there are certain topics and people who are not, and never will be, suitable for literary treatment; Tolstoy's hero Polikushka, Fet notes with regret, is just such an artistic nonstarter. He then elaborates:

> Why do you, trying to oblige the artistic search for the new, allow yourself to look for it in the rot? You'll tell me that I have no sense of smell, and that nothing's rotten here. . . . [But] the barbarous people cannot have

a history, and no one can force it to have something that doesn't exist. The mold of the people cannot, that is to say, must not have its own story-teller. And the right of our former household serfs to the pen of a first-class writer is even less than that of the most loathsome Negroes (look at Uncle Tom). The peasants are a different matter: they may be barbarians, but they are humans. Household serfs are not humans but are incomprehen-sibly clad in a garb of pretensions to humanity. And what's the result? You strove with all your strength to reach a point unreachable by God, you wanted to be an aloof judge and ended up, as it were, in the lawyers' back row. This is painful for me![33]

Painful, indeed![34] But what is fascinating about Fet's yelp of rage is the way it shifts emphasis away from the "tendentious" aspects of *Uncle Tom* and of "Polikushka" toward the sheer impertinence of literature about the "barbarous people." As with some later naturalist (e.g., Zola) and modernist (e.g., Joyce) literature, the real, underlying scandal of these works lies not in any obvious attempt to affect political life but in their (inherently political) undoing of existing regimes of representa-tion, their decision to place "rot" on the stage.

Yet Tolstoy—whether out of dissatisfaction with the story, respect for Fet, or some degree of genuine agreement with the poet's stand— apparently accepted this critique, replying on 1–3 May 1863:

> Well, who was it anyway who wrote . . . "Polikushka"? What's the point of discussing [it]. Paper tolerates anything [written on it], and the editor pays for everything and prints it. . . . You're correct, of course, but after all there aren't many readers like you. "Polikushka" is just idle chatter on the first subject that came to the mind of a person who also happens to "wield a skillful pen."[35]

Tolstoy doesn't exactly rush to assent to Fet's more general argument, limiting his agreement to the question of "Polikushka" alone; this suggests that he was both trying to avoid conflict and (more likely, perhaps) rather bored with the whole thing. He concurs with Fet again a few years later when, in a letter criticizing Turgenev's *Smoke* as mere polemic, the poet makes reference to Stowe's novel, here cast in the more familiar role of foremost representative of the "tendentious": "In an artistic work, intensity is a matter of great importance. But it must be located near the center [of the work], and not from some outside periphery. The stronger it tends toward the center, the better—as in *Hamlet*, *Faust*, *Macbeth*. The more intensely it emanates from the outside, the uglier, the sicklier, the worse the work is. *Uncle Tom* and the like."[36]

Thirteen days later, Tolstoy replied simply, "I wanted to write to you long ago about *Smoke* and, of course, to write exactly what you've written to me."[37] Whether Tolstoy actually agreed with Fet or not in 1867, it is clear that he had changed his mind by the early 1880s, around which time (in the wake of his famous religious crisis) he turned both to writing and publishing for "the people" and to polemical writing against militarism, patriotism, the use of money and tobacco, the consumption of meat, private property, and a host of other features of mainstream life. Both of Fet's comments suggest that *Uncle Tom's Cabin* is offensive to the extent that it transgresses boundaries, whether by breaking limits of "decorum" and subject matter or by opening itself up to social intensities "emanating from the outside." In both these respects, the work of the later Tolstoy could hardly be more at odds with Fet's notion of art and the artist, though quite consonant with aspects of Stowe's achievement.

And this affinity shows in a couple of scattered remarks Tolstoy made during this late period. On 9 October 1891 he wrote an appreciative letter to the famous Austrian antiwar writer and activist Bertha von Suttner (1843–1914; winner of the 1905 Nobel Peace Prize), whose *Lay Down Your Arms* (*Die Waffen nieder*) had been published to sensational acclaim two years earlier. His congratulation situates Suttner's work as a successor to that of Stowe: "The abolition of slavery [in the United States] was preceded by a famous book written by a woman, Mrs. Stowe; may God grant that the abolition of war is achieved through yours."[38] But Stowe, the morally effective writer nonpareil, also provided a model for what Tolstoy himself wished to achieve at this stage. Thus in a diary entry from 9 August 1894, he sets himself yet another monumental literary-ethical task: "[Varvara] MacGahan came by . . . with her son and brought books from Henry George. I read once more *A Perplexed Philosopher*. Wonderful. Again I had a sharp realization of the sin of land ownership. It's amazing how people don't see this. How necessary it would be to write about this—to write a new *Uncle Tom's Cabin*."[39] Tolstoy never wrote an antiownership *Uncle Tom's Cabin*, but it is clear that *Uncle Tom* provided Tolstoy an important instance of a literature that might truly and effectively convey "sentiments which arise . . . in relation to God and to our neighbor." His admiration was complete by the time he said in the 1890s (in communication with his translator and biographer Aylmer Maude):

A great literature is born when an elevated moral sentiment is awoken. Take, for example, the period of the emancipation movements—the struggle for the abolition of serfdom in Russia, and the struggle for the liberation of the Negroes in the United States. Look at the writers who appeared at that time in America: Harriet Beecher Stowe, Thoreau, Emerson, Lowell, Whittier, Longfellow, William Lloyd Garrison, Theodore Parker, and others. And in Russia: Dostoevsky, Turgenev, Herzen, and others, whose influence on the educated circles of society was very great.[40]

Here Tolstoy both offers a rough heuristic for future comparison of the two "movements" and alludes to his ongoing attempts to make that atmosphere of "elevated moral sentiment" something permanent. And indeed, the grand "public sphere" of moral inquiry and pedagogical influence he constructed (usually called "Tolstoyanism") was in no small way responsible for maintaining and extending the importance of Stowe's novel for the rapidly increasing numbers of Russians attaining literacy in the late nineteenth–early twentieth centuries.

This began, in fact, well before the 1880s. Tolstoy opened a school for peasants on his estate of Yasnaya Polyana in 1859, and after intensive studies of contemporary educational theory founded and contributed articles to a journal (called *Yasnaya Polyana*) devoted to elaboration and propagation of his ideas about pedagogy.[41] In 1862, an adaptation and abridgement of *Uncle Tom's Cabin* by Mitrofan Fedorovich Butovich, a teacher closely involved with both the school and the journal, was published as a supplement.[42] Adapted from the *Russian Messenger* translation, Butovich's is apparently the first explicit "reworking" of the novel to appear in Russia. Although the basics of the story are kept, virtually all the debate in the novel is removed—presaging many later versions for children—and while the setting remains "America," many of the character names are converted into Russian-sounding ones: Eliza becomes Maria, George becomes Aleksandr, little Harry becomes Vaniatka, George Shelby becomes Grisha, and Tom's kids (Mose and Pete) become Klimka and Vas'ka. The Russianizing of the text extends to the use of native diminutives, as when Aunt Chloe (who gets to keep her name) cries out "Oh, my Tomushka, they're taking you away from me."[43] Clearly, Butovich was intent on smoothing the reception of the story by peasant readers through substituting odd names like "Harry" with something more familiar. We occasionally find similar garnishes of "local" detail as late as 1917; in an edition of that year, George Harris becomes "Egor," Andy "Andrei," and Tom refers to his master Shelby by the Russian term *barin*.[44]

The report of the censor (one A. Smirnov) who examined and approved Butovich's version survives, and it casts fascinating light on the way at least one educated cultural authority conceived of the book's possible reception by the "people." Butovich's version tries, writes the censor, to use "words typical of the everyday discourse of our former serfs, [so that] the simple person can easily apply everything that is narrated about American slaves to his own former enserfed existence."[45] This might seem to entertain dangerously provocative comparisons, especially given the persistence of peasant discontent over the emancipation settlement. "But," adds Smirnov, "because in the narrative under consideration slaveholders and especially ladies and children are represented as humane (only . . . slave traders are shown to be cruel-hearted), the story cannot, in my opinion, provoke hostile feelings among the peasants to their former owners. Thus, inasmuch as the caste of [slave traders] . . . did not exist among us at all, so our former serfs can still feel the great superiority of their former situation relative to that of American Negroes."[46]

Thus a significant social (but not *ethnic*) difference, and one central to the novel's plot, is judged as sufficient to defuse any explosive analogies that a peasant reader might make. The world of *Uncle Tom's Cabin* is familiar enough to be fascinating, alien enough to be contrasted to rather than identified with Russian reality, but the novel has another virtue beyond the interest generated by its representation of bondage:

> What is especially of interest in this story for our simple people is the model of Uncle Tom, a Negro slave, a person religious to the highest degree, who never parts with his Bible and with equanimity endures his heavy lot, in accord with Holy Scripture, in expectation of the heavenly kingdom. . . . An acquaintance with this kind of figure, and adopting his path, is especially desirable for our poorly provided-for, simple people.[47]

Taken together, Smirnov's comments prefigure some central facets of the book's reception by the religious (and in part Tolstoyan) section of the prerevolutionary educated elite. The insistence on the book's appeal to universal feelings and sympathies remains, but the comparison with Russian serfdom as such begins to recede; apart from the obligatory references to the novel's appearance in Russian "on the eve of the emancipation," *Uncle Tom* becomes a more *American* book, in a reading in tune (as we have seen) with British uses of Stowe to critique the United States, but which will reach full fruition only in the Soviet period.[48] On the other hand, the idea that the "Negro slave" Uncle Tom is an ideal role model for the "simple people"—in his piety, his pacifism, and his striving for literacy—will become dominant in late nineteenth-century reception, only to be largely thrust aside by a post-1917 cultural order with rather different protocols for heroism.

As I have already indicated, *Uncle Tom's Cabin* also turns into a work of "children's literature" around this time, in Russia as elsewhere; indeed, it seems that Russians adopted Stowe's novel as a children's book partially in imitation of practices in Europe and the United States.[49] In one of the most important early overviews of children's literature in Russia, the pedagogue N. V. Chekhov identified sentimentalism, romances of family life (Louisa May Alcott's *Little Women*, prototypically), and narratives with national or "folk" coloration (everything from fairy tales to Tolstoy's peasant pedagogy) as the main genre tributaries converging into the mainstream of children's literature in Russia, and it is not difficult to see how *Uncle Tom's Cabin*—a sentimental, domestic, and rural novel all at once—satisfies those rubrics.[50] We might add to this mix, although Chekhov does not, that current of high idealism injected early on into Russian children's literature by critic Vissarion Belinsky, who insisted that writing for the young must not be merely diverting, but also "acquaint [children] with the mystery of suffering, presenting it as another side of . . . love, as a blessing of its kind; not as an unpleasant contingency, but as a necessary condition of spirit."[51]

The metamorphosis is not total, to be sure, and as the censor Smirnov recommends, the book received ongoing endorsement as suitable fare for adults learning to read, peasants in particular. Conveniently enough, the text itself seems to welcome readers of varying age, not least in the way that (as Alessandro Portelli has pointed out) the age of its central protagonist feels protean: Tom is at once father and valued servant in the prime of life, glowing with childlike faith, and wise and esteemed patriarch.[52]

Chekhov makes the additional fascinating observation that children's literature in Russia needs to be conceptualized at the crossroads of literature for adults, on the one hand, and ideas about pedagogy, on the other, and I would surmise that adult peasant readers might have been situated (by the elites) at a nearby intersection. Although literature for children had existed in Russia since the mid-eighteenth century, the postemancipation years brought about a reevaluation of the previous era's children's books and journals—mostly destined for sons and daughters of relatively privileged families—and an outpouring of descriptions of, advice for, and statistics about Russia's new readerships, especially peasants and young people.[53] Tolstoy's *Yasnaya Polyana* was one of the earliest responses to this situation, and it would be worthwhile to examine (although I cannot do so here, regrettably) contemporary Russian works on reading to see just how much the categories of "peasant" and "child" overlapped from the pedagogues', journalists', or bureaucrats' perspectives. At any rate, the same reasons seem to have made *Uncle Tom's Cabin* "suitable" for peasants and for children: its provision of good models of conduct; the window it offered onto US history; its status as esteemed world classic, aesthetic shortcomings notwithstanding; the simplicity, excitement, and emotional intensity of its story.

To be sure, writers like Tolstoy and Butovich were intervening in a highly complex, mutable postemancipation social situation, in which the lives of the "simple people" were far from settled or idyllic. Class divisions persisted, terrible famines (especially in 1891–92) and epidemics ravaged the countryside, and population growth (of 25 percent between 1877 and 1905) exacerbated both the land shortage and discontent over persisting gross inequities of ownership—by 1905, 12 million peasant households together held approximately twice the total amount of land owned by 100,000 noble estates.[54] Yet there was no Jim Crow in Russia; it was easier for former serfs, and certainly for the children and grandchildren of serfs, to move out of the peasant milieu into other social and geographical spaces than it was for the descendants of slaves in the United States. The new relative mobility (which should not be exaggerated) generated its own problems, as that urban proletariat Khomyakov had so dreaded started to take shape; as radical ideas began to spread; as newly literate peasants began to read secular, commercial writing; and (in general) as older sources of cultural authority, religious and otherwise, began to lose their grip on the population.[55] It was into this breach that a variety of projects to condition the culture of the emergent "new" population entered (including government-sponsored cultural centers and libraries)—and Stowe's novel, with its pious, gentle hero, had its small role to play in all of this.

We know from the records of circulating libraries and other evidence that *Uncle Tom's Cabin* became a mainstay for Russian readers after 1880, but why did Stowe's book attain the success it did?[56] In her study of *Uncle Tom* in France, Edith Lucas suggests that the novel's popularity in that country might have had something to do with the way it articulated and preserved reformist or even revolutionary hopes after the defeats of 1848, but in a Christian or "mystical socialist" guise, with any political irritants subdued (if not removed) by religious eschatology.[57] In the Russian case, we might speculate that *Uncle Tom's Cabin* functioned as a kind of "vanishing mediator" for the rapidly expanding postemanci-pation reading public, and specifically for the peasantry, in the way it blended religious writing—the major interest of peasant readers in the middle of the century, though not by the end—with secular forms like those of the adventure story, melodrama, the historical novel, and the "literary classic" as such.[58] (Indeed, some prerevolutionary Russian editions managed to pare the text down into a very effective adventure narrative, minus description and dialectic.)[59] As far as the elites are concerned, it is easy enough to see how *Uncle Tom* managed to answer demands issuing from very disparate quarters: from liberals concerned with social injustice, to radicals questioning capitalism and market rela-tions (the book evidently was one of Lenin's favorites, at least in child-hood), to conservatives concerned about sustaining the culture's Christian center, and finally, and not least, men of the book trade on the lookout for material that would sell.[60]

In 1884, Tolstoy, in collaboration with his disciple Vladimir Grigorie-vich Chertkov (1854–1936) and the publisher Ivan Dmitrievich Sytin (1851–1934) started Posrédnik (Intermediary), a publishing house de-voted to releasing books that combined the appeal of the new "commer-cial" literature with morally edifying content, including proverbs and works by Tolstoy and writers with Tolstoyan leanings. It proved a highly successful venture, and Sytin became one of the most important pub-lishers of the age.[61] Already in its first year, the Sytin publishing house put out a much-condensed and simplified version of *Uncle Tom's Cabin*. The adaptation contains a statement of editorial purpose: "The goal of the publishers is to distribute genuinely good books among the people through the means provided by schools, the army, and peddlers; to give the people healthy and rational nourishment; and to oppose specu-lation in books and illiterate publishers of *luboks* [cheap commercial books]."[62]

From 1897 until 1925 the director of Posrednik was Ivan Ivanovich Gorbunov-Posadov (1864–1940), a follower of Tolstoy and later advo-cate of radical "free educational" pedagogical ideas.[63] Gorbunov-Posadov began Sytin's major series Library for Children and Youth, and it was in this series in 1902 that Gorbunov-Posadov published an edition of *Uncle Tom's Cabin* with a long afterword by himself. This essay, titled "The Liberators of the Black Slaves," gives remarkable in-sight into the somewhat contradictory attitudes of one significant

branch of the educated elite toward slavery, toward the United States
and Africa, and toward the social function of literature as a path to both
"right conduct" and literacy.

Though Gorbunov-Posadov touches on many aspects of slavery and
postslavery—and covers a huge historical span, from precolonial
African times to America's Jim Crow present—his appreciation of
Stowe's novel is the centerpiece. Certainly, his report of a "typical"
reading experience can stand with any of the strongest testimonies to
the book's affective power:

> Although [what Stowe describes] happened so long ago, when reading
> this book one still goes through the whole life of those black outcasts and
> suffers with them all of their suffering over again. On their behalf tears of
> pity and resentment rise into the throat, the entire soul overflows with
> indignation toward their pitiless oppressors, and one wants with all one's
> heart to defend them, save them, seize them out of bondage. Then you
> come back to yourself and say: "But isn't all of that in the past? It is no
> more! Thank God, thank God! But why did it ever exist, why did brother
> humans torment their fellows in this way? Why did they allow such a
> crime to be realized on earth?" If this book has such an effect on us now,
> after slavery has long vanished from the face of America, with what
> strength it must have struck the hearts of those people who lived side by
> side with slavery, with those who committed their dastardly acts?[64]

Indeed, Gorbunov-Posadov maintains (in an obviously Tolstoyan
argument) that it was through the writings of "the great advocates of
freedom," and not "through the rifles and cannons of the victors," that
true liberation for the slaves was achieved.[65] Before *Uncle Tom's Cabin*,
he writes, (white) Americans had thought of Africans as "half-humans,
half-animals, destined to obey the white race." Through reading it they
learned that the black person "is not only equal to the white person in
all things, but that he might be infinitely superior to the white people
around him. Although they are many whites living in Tom's vicinity
who call themselves Christians, only Tom, the black slave, is a true
Christian—only he clearly understands the teachings of Christ and
confesses, expresses them in his entire being."[66] Undergirding this
response (which no doubt would have met with Stowe's approval) is
the whole Tolstoyan idealization of the "wise passivity" of the Russian
peasant—Gerasim in "The Death of Ivan Ilych," Platon Karatayev in
War and Peace—as well as a bit of sincerely meant encouragement for
peasant students embarked on the difficult road to enlightenment.
(Stowe herself, to whom Gorbunov-Posadov devotes an entire section

of the essay, is portrayed as another example of the humble achieving the great through hard work, and therefore worthy of emulation.)

Indeed, this new vision of the wise slave (or ex-slave) is quite perceptible in the way that certain Tolstoyan versions of *Uncle Tom's Cabin* alter parts of Stowe's text. A particularly striking example appears in a *Yasnaya Polyana* edition from 1903, in which Tom and Little Eva read and discuss Scripture together, and Tom is made far more the teacher than in Stowe's original:

> While walking with Little Eva, Tom told her stories from Holy Scripture: about the creation of the world; about Cain killing Abel; about marvelous Joseph, sold by his brothers into Egypt; about Moses and the freeing of the Jews from Babylonian captivity; and about Christ the Savior, his sufferings; and about much besides. Eva had no teacher: no one spoke to her about God, his divine Son, about Christ's teachings. Tom told these stories in an engaging way, and Eva listened to him with interest.[67]

This revision, also reflected in some of the illustrations of this classic scene in the Russian editions of the novel—which depict Tom as adult pedagogue, with Eva listening—essentially inverts the Tom-Eva intellectual hierarchy as Stowe established it (fig. 1).[68]

It is worth mentioning in passing here that these alterations might reflect broader differences separating American and Russian attitudes toward the capacities of former bondspeople, as evidenced by the contrast between the textbooks written for freedpeople in the two countries postemancipation. In the Russian texts—not least the ones produced by Tolstoy, starting in the late 1850s—peasants are often depicted as major and relatively autonomous contributors to the national fund of knowledge and value, as possessing a rationality that must be credited as such. The majority of US freedman's primers, by contrast, represent blacks as empty vessels to be filled, as grateful recipients of white benevolence and learning. That is, Russian peasants, including ex-serfs, are represented as already involved in the building of a "national culture," rather than as (always already) having to be brought into that culture.[69]

We are dealing with idealization and "romantic nationalism" here, to be sure, and these contrasts might be striking in relative terms only. As historian Cathy Frierson has demonstrated, a persistent array of "educated" stereotypes about the Russian peasantry and various presumed subsections of it (the greedy *kulak*, or wealthy peasant; the categories of either "virago, shrew, or victim" to which peasant women

Figure 1. From *Khizhina diadi Toma, ili belye i chernye*, ed. P. P. Shcheglov (Moscow: Vil'e, 1896).

were invariably assigned; and several others) emerged and structured the way peasant life was investigated and represented in the latter half of the nineteenth century.[70] Thus, late-Tolstoyan celebrations of the wisdom of freedpeople are probably better thought of as positions taken in a sprawling, complex battle over peasant representation.

Nor by any means does the balance of value swing entirely to the advantage of former US slaves in the Russian texts, which follow Euro-American models all too frequently. Gorbunov-Posadov makes it clear at the beginning of his article that the cultural *Erbe* of the African slaves is drastically inferior to that of the West, and it would seem that the potential for spiritual superiority is only partial compensation for a colossal initial lag:

> The life of African Negroes is poor and benighted. They do not know the spiritual needs and delights that exist among enlightened peoples; they do not know the elevated delight of an acquaintance with the works of

great thinkers, poets, and scholars; they do not know the joys of knowing the most exalted revelations of human wisdom, which point humanity toward ever newer, higher paths and goals. . . . Almost nothing of all of this has, up to our time, been a part of the Negro's life. To a large extent his main pleasure amounts to eating well, and sometimes to get drunk on some sort of intoxicating drink.[71]

Gorbunov-Posadov never identifies the source of his information about Africa; the last remark about fondness for "intoxicating drink" suggests that he might be projecting notions about certain Russian peasant practices into his representation of "benighted" Africans. Again, we might make reference here to some of the Russian *Tom* illustrations, which not infrequently represent blacks in a distinctly cartoonish and dehumanized manner, directly derived or even copied from imported stereotypes to be sure, and in sharp contrast to a much less stylized, more "unmarked" and realistic depiction (also imported) of whites and "quadroons" (fig. 2).[72] Indeed, in Russia as elsewhere, George and (especially) Eliza Harris are often made white, if also given a vaguely orientalized appearance (fig. 3), in a tradition that persists through the overwhelming majority of Soviet editions as well. In one particularly striking illustration from a 1917 Sytin edition (fig. 4), set in the slave warehouse (vol. 2, chap. 30 of the novel), the near-white Susan and her daughter Emmeline are represented as the only figures in the crowd of otherwise black slaves reacting emotionally—that is, in a way with which readers could identify—to the horrific spectacle around them, although admittedly the illustrator follows Stowe here in focusing on the "piously instructed and trained" mulatto mother and quadroon daughter and their feelings (Stowe, 337). Overall, one detects a constant, stark, if typical tension in the *Uncle Tom* illustrations between relatively realistic but "whitened" portrayals and minstrelized "darky" caricature. Intriguingly, depictions of Uncle Tom in Russian editions often show him, especially in moments of sadness, with his hands covering his face, as if in melancholy confirmation of Marcus Wood's observation (here in reference to George Cruikshank's early illustrations of the novel) that "[the problem of deciding] whether Tom was to be drawn with the traditional features of an Anglo-Saxon hero or as a grinning Blackface, there being no stylistic middle ground, was never resolved."[73]

To be sure, Gorbunov-Posadov's contradictory representation of Africans as at once "inferior" and worthy of emulation both reflects something in Stowe's own ideology and reveals, I think, a tension latent

Figure 2. From *Khizhina diadi Toma, ili belye i chernye (po Bicher-Stou)*, 4th ed. (Moscow: Evdokiia Konovalova, 1917); based on illustrations by A. S. Forrest in *Uncle Tom's Cabin* [from the Stories Told to Children series], ed. H. E. Marshall (Edinburgh: T. C. Jack, 1904). The original caption of the image on the left reads, "'You really don't love anyone, Topsy?' asked Eva. 'I don't know anything about love,' answered the Negro girl Topsy." In the original caption of the image on the right, Eliza says, "You know, Uncle Tom, Aunt Chloe wants to pay for your redemption. Poor Chloe!"

Figure 3. Cover image of *Khizhina diadi Toma*, trans. E. B. [Posrednik ed.] (Moscow: I. N. Kushnerev, 1908).

Figure 4. From *Khizhina diadi Toma (po Bicher-Stou)* (Moscow: Sytin, 1917). The original caption reads, "The buyers unceremoniously inspected the goods, pricing human beings as though they were horses."

in the ameliorative projects of the educated elites more generally. For them, "modernization" is necessary, but premodern ways of life must be respected and even valorized at once as a kind of corrective to enlightened hubris; as vital repositories of and sources for the emerging "national" culture; and in order to paper over the deep rift of condescension enabling the elites to treat slaves or freedpeople as objects of "analysis" in the first place.

Perhaps this is one of the reasons why the stereotyped dramatic subgenre of the "mortgage melodrama"—classically, where a destitute family fearfully anticipates the mortgage on the ancestral property coming due (sometimes on Christmas Eve), until the last-minute rescue by a relative or retainer, who arrives on the scene with the cash—enjoyed considerable popularity in both the United States (in "saving-the-old-plantation" stories by Thomas Nelson Page, for instance) and Russia (most famously and ironically in Anton Chekhov's *Cherry Orchard* [1904]) during these years.[74] This subgenre enables a passionate though not necessarily stable coordination of nostalgia and claims to possession with an acceptance of socioeconomic change.[75] (Of course, *Uncle Tom's Cabin* is also an ironic inversion of the mortgage melodrama—perhaps one of the earliest and most fraught.)

At any rate, attitudes of both sentimental admiration and patronizing paternalism become plainly visible later in Gorbunov-Posadov's essay, when cultural racism is used as a background against which the efforts of emancipated slaves to become educated shine forth:

> [In the school] a sixty-year-old pupil diligently traced out letters with his pen, and next to him a small, blackish little boy with a spread-out nose labored over his ABCs. With burning enthusiasm the Negroes were working here, overcoming the first difficulties on the road to knowledge. The teachers, men and women, also put their entire souls into their work, as they try to convert the slavish, fearful mentality of the blacks into the rational, bright, free consciousness of an independent person.[76]

These and related representations had staying power, to be sure: thirty years later, while working in Moscow as a consultant on an abortive Comintern-sponsored film about US race relations, Langston Hughes was appalled to discover that the Russian scenarist had evidently taken his "characterization of Negro manners and mentality . . . from *Uncle Tom's Cabin*."[77] At the same time, of Gorbunov-Posadov's seriousness about the "potential" and achievements of former slaves—he speaks glowingly of Frederick Douglass, in a rare Russian mention—there can be no doubt. This is particularly clear in the essay's concluding section, which is one of the earliest truly frank accounts in Russian of American racial barriers: of Jim Crow, the terrorizing of blacks by the Ku Klux Klan, lynching, and even the relationship of European racism to ongoing colonial oppression.[78] The Enlightenment Eurocentrism of Gorbunov-Posadov's general attitude does not prevent him, in the end, from vigorously castigating the contemporary United States for its ongoing suppression of African Americans—"*white* Americans" continue to require education, and thus Stowe's task remains an "unfinished" one.

The contrast with the US reception of the novel at this time is striking: beginning around 1892 (when Stowe's copyright expired), *Uncle Tom's Cabin* was reprinted more often and more cheaply, and was more exploited for commercial purposes, than ever before in the Jim Crow United States.[79] Meanwhile, works of a starkly opposing ideological character—such as Thomas Dixon's bestselling, racist anti-*Tom* novel, *The Leopard's Spots*, published the same year as Gorbunov-Posadov's afterword (1902)—won enormous attention and acclaim, thereby trumping Stowe's novel, now degraded through condensation, cartoon, and commodification, in the "seriousness and relevance" stakes. At the same time, textual and (especially) visual iconography deriving from *Uncle Tom's Cabin* was quietly recoded into nostalgic and anti-abolitionist terms in the late nineteenth century, so that Stowe's hero became "an apologist for the Lost Cause, and a spokesman for the New South."[80]

That *Uncle Tom's Cabin* was by now established as an "old classic" served to domesticate and neutralize it as well, even as this canonical status crucially helped make more scrupulous and thoughtful readings possible through the grimmest years of US racist reaction. African American writers ranging from Frederick Douglass and Charles Chesnutt to W. E. B. Du Bois and James Weldon Johnson praised Stowe's achievement during these years—both as a contrast to the squalors of Dixon and his like and because other public textual occasions for reflection on slavery, such as slave narratives, were unavailable or forgotten— even as the seeds of a later, dialectical African American critique of Stowe simultaneously became visible.[81] Much more writing about peasant life during and after serfdom would have been available in Russia, of course; and it seems likely that *Uncle Tom's Cabin* was received there primarily as a fount of ethical example, on the one hand, and as a source of (sobering) knowledge about the United States and its history, on the other.[82]

The sense of participating in an *ongoing* ethical project is probably useful to keep in mind when evaluating the Russian translations that appeared during this period under the auspices of the reformist/religious literate elites. Virtually all the references in Stowe's text to white superiority, Anglo-Saxonism, and so on are simply, quietly removed from the 1902 version in which Gorbunov-Posadov's essay appears. This kind of (partial) "de-racializing" was especially true of adaptations for children, which were often drastically condensed (one 1910 edition is only twenty-four pages long), but is evident in less altered versions as well, as in this 1916 translation by A. M. Vit:[83]

> There stood the two children, representatives of the two extremes of society. The fair, high-bred child, with her golden head, her deep eyes, her spiritual, noble brow, and prince-like movements; and her black, keen, subtle, cringing, yet acute neighbor. They stood the representatives of their races. The Saxon, born of ages of cultivation, command, education, physical and moral eminence; the Afric, born of ages of oppression, submission, ignorance, toil, and vice! (Stowe, 254)

> Both [Topsy and Eva] sat on the floor, turned slightly away from [St. Clare]: Topsy, with her usual careless look, Eva with her flaming cheeks and tears in her eyes.[84]

Other translators make more ambivalent decisions. In L. A. Murakhina's 1912 rendering of the same passage, Topsy's "inferiority" is more explicitly ascribed to the fact of slavery, but the translator fails to interpret Eva's "superiority" in the same historical/environmental terms, while not granting Topsy even those strengths of subtlety and acuity that Stowe allows her:

> It is difficult to imagine a sharper contrast than that of these two girls standing face to face. Delicate, elegant, blonde, and fair Eva, shot through with the nobility of the higher race; and black, ugly Topsy, with all the characteristics of a being whose ancestors had been in slavery, with all of its terrible consequences: ignorance, vice, and poverty.[85]

Sometimes the alterations are more drastic and remarkable. Frequently, Stowe's final chapter ("Concluding Remarks") is excised from Russian translations beginning in the early 1900s, no doubt because of its topical, presumably time-bound abolitionist message. An earlier Sytin edition (also translated by Murakhina), however, complexly alters the very last section of the original in order to bring Stowe's critique up-to-date as a reflection on contemporary America:

But who may abide the day of his appearing? "for that day shall burn as an oven: and he shall appears as a swift witness against those that oppress the hireling in his wages, the widow and the fatherless, and that *turn aside the stranger in his right*: and he shall break in pieces the oppressor."

Are not these dread words for a nation bearing in her bosom so mighty an injustice? Christians! every time that you pray that the kingdom of Christ may come, can you forget that prophecy associates, in dread fellowship, the *day of vengeance* with the year of his redeemed?

Cont. p. 58

And you, Christians, do you not tremble each time you pray for the coming of His kingdom, when you yourselves oppose that coming with all your strength, by committing or at least allowing the most scandalous crimes against the Holy Spirit?!

And you, *free* America, remember that you can save yourself from the Lord's anger only if you repent of your misdeeds and return to the path of Christian charity and justice. The laws of the highest morality are as immutable as those of nature—by whose power every crime carries with it a corresponding punishment. . . . Remember this, if you want to cleanse

Cont. p. 58

A day of grace is yet held out to us. Both North and South have been guilty before God; and the Christian church has a heavy account to answer. Not by combining together, to protect injustice and cruelty, and making a common capital of sin, is this Union to be saved,—but by repentance, justice and mercy; for, not surer is the eternal law by which the millstone sinks in the ocean, than that stronger law, by which injustice and cruelty shall bring on nations the wrath of Almighty God! (Stowe, 456)

yourself in the eyes of other nations, and save yourself from eternal judgment!

You have been given time to repent—use it, before it is too late! Remember that it has been said: "for that day will burn, [etc.]."[86]

Repent, America, shake off those fetters by means of which you, in ruining others, ruin yourself even more! Be a follower of the Gospel not only in word but in deed, and only then will you be able to await without fear the second glorious coming of the Savior of the world.[87]

Stowe's attack on the Fugitive Slave Law—on North and South "combining together, to protect injustice and cruelty"—is turned into a critique of "*free* America's" ongoing "fettering" of "others." It is implied that the criticism is leveled on behalf of "other nations," whose censure is placed on almost the same level with "eternal judgment"; again, the internationalism of this ethical work (of the educated elite) is stressed. Jim Crow is never mentioned, leaving open an extension of the reproach to some of America's colonial adventures (in particular, perhaps, in the Philippines [1899-1902] and Panama [1902-3]), but the central, domestic-American target of Murakhina's revision remains clear.[88] On the level of religious sentiment, Stowe's apocalypticism is softened, replaced by the less baleful admonition to help and not hinder the coming of God's kingdom on earth—whose arrival Tolstoyans like Murakhina hoped would be abetted by their own educational "deeds."

The most astonishing manifestation of the effects of the crusading mentality of the educated elites on their apprehension of Stowe's work is found in the 1912 Murakhina translation of the "Henrique" chapter, in which the character of Augustine St. Clare undergoes a striking mutation. The passage really needs to be compared with the original, part of which I have quoted already, investigating a different crux of translation (I have set off the important alterations in italics in the Murakhina):

"Because," said Alfred, "we can see plainly enough that all men are

"If I [Alfred] were to take it into my head to convince Henrique [i.e., his

not born free, nor born equal; they are born anything else. For my part, I think half this republican talk sheer humbug. It is the educated, the intelligent, the wealthy, the refined, who ought to have equal rights, and not the canaille."

"If you can keep the canaille of that opinion," said Augustine. "They took *their* turn once, in France."

"Of course, they must be kept down, consistently, steadily, as I *should*," said Alfred, setting his foot hard down, as if he were standing on somebody.

"It makes a terrible slip when they get up," said Augustine,—"in St. Domingo, for instance."

"Poh!" said Alfred, "we'll take care of that, in this country. We must set our face against all this educating, elevating talk, that is getting about now; the lower class must not be educated."

"That is past praying for," said Augustine; "educated they will be, and we have only to say how. Our system is educating them in barbarism and brutality. We are breaking all humanizing ties, and making them brute beasts; and, if they get the upper hand, such we shall find them."

"They never shall get the upper hand!" said Alfred.

[. . .]

"I tell you," said Augustine, "if there is anything that is revealed with the strength of a divine law in our times, it is that the masses are to rise, and the under class become the upper one."

son] of the existence of this 'equality,' he'd be fully in his rights if he laughed directly in my face. Only people who are all well educated, intelligent, and rich are equal to one another, just as people of lower races and layers of society are equal—to one another.

"All of that concerns external appearances alone, but all are equal in soul."

"That's not true, either, Augustine. If 'souls' were equal, they would manifest themselves in the same way, but that, after all, doesn't happen."[89]

"No, because one part of the souls oppresses the other part. But before God, all the same, all are equal."

"Before God? Since when did you grow keen on theology?"

"Do you really think that to acknowledge the existence of God amounts to becoming keen on theology? Your people are subdivided into classes; you go and ask your bondsmen if they think that's just. Watch, brother, that all those who are still obeying you—that is, more precisely, who are obeying your stick—won't someday come to the conclusion that if they unite all their power, it won't cost them anything to rip the stick out of your hands and use it on you."

"Don't worry, Augustine, I and people like me know how to forestall all possibility of such 'conclusions.' Thus, for example, at present has risen up a mania for spreading education among the masses. We understand that this is bad for the masses and try to oppose it with all our strength."

"Real enlightenment is still not suited to the masses, for the masses are not prepared for it. The time to begin that

Cont. p. 60

Cont. p. 60

"That's one of your red republican humbugs, Augustine! Why didn't you ever take to the stump;—you'd make a famous stump orator! Well, I hope I shall be dead before this millennium of your greasy masses comes on."

"Greasy or not greasy, they will govern you, when their time comes," said Augustine; "and they will be just such rulers as you make them. The French noblesse chose to have the people 'sans culottes,' and had 'sans culottes' governors to their hearts' content. The people of Hayti—"

"O, come, Augustine! as if we hadn't had enough of that abominable, contemptible Hayti! The Haytiens were not Anglo Saxons; if they had been, there would have been another story. The Anglo Saxon is the dominant race of the world, and *is to be so.*"

"Well, there is a pretty fair infusion of Anglo Saxon blood among our slaves, now," said Augustine. "There are plenty among them who have only enough of the African to give a sort of tropical warmth and fervor to our calculating firmness and fore-sight. If ever the San Domingo hour comes, Anglo Saxon blood will lead on the day. Sons of white fathers, with all our haughty feelings burning in their veins, will not always be bought and sold and traded. They will rise, and raise with them their mother's race."

"Stuff!—nonsense!"

"Well," said Augustine, "there goes an old saying to this effect 'As it was in the days of Noah, so shall it be;—they ate, they drank, they planted, they builded, and knew not till the flood came and took them.'"

preparation has arrived, and in that every honest person is obliged to participate. Our own interests demand as much. Up till now, we've developed all sorts of bad instincts among the people, and if someday those beasts take from us the upper hand—which I believe is very possible. . . ."

"Perhaps. But in any event, we're still very far from that," noted Alfred.

"On the contrary: judging by certain signs that only someone who deliberately closes his eyes does not see, this catastrophe is very near. . . . The only way to avert it is to try to raise the lower classes to one's own level."

"There you go again! Understand, Augustine, that in the end you're preach-ing utopia. After all, it's just as if you said that we have to try to make sure that all people are of the same height! But that's impossible. . . . Negroes are in no way suited to power; the superior role is destined for the Anglo-Saxon race alone. . . ."

"And for your part, you should know that a very goodly amount of Anglo-Saxon blood flows in the veins of our slaves, *blood that we took pains to pour into them.* When that hour strikes, the one that made San Domingo free from white influence, then you'll know that that entire movement will be led precisely by Anglo-Saxon blood."

"That will never happen here."

"Oh yes, people in Noah's time also didn't want to believe that some-day would arrive the day of reckoning for their sins."

"Well, Augustine, our flood, in truth, is still far in the future, I assure you. If

"On the whole, Augustine, I think your talents might do for a circuit rider," said Alfred, laughing. "Never you fear for us; possession is our nine points. We've got the power. This subject race," said he, stamping firmly, "is down, and shall stay down! We have energy enough to manage our own powder." (Stowe, 275–77) *you're counting on becoming a second Noah, you're in for a bitter disappointment.* This ignoble race," added Alfred, stamping his foot, "must be below us and will remain there forever! *We had the intelligence to invent gunpowder— we've got the intelligence to put it into action for our own benefit.*"[90]

It proves fairly simple (though still requiring actual additions *to*, rather than mere alterations *of* the original) to turn St. Clare into a spokesman for the reformist-religious elite. Both his debate with those who regard any form of social improvement as utopian and his insistence on the moral duty of participation reveal how this discourse is embedded in the values and identity of Russia's educated elites. The contradictions of that worldview are made apparent as well, in the copresence of sympathy for the downtrodden and criticism of oppression (especially in the observation that the slaveholders actually "took pains" to "pour" their blood into the slaves) with apparent acceptance of "Saxonist" ideology, a firm belief in the cultural inferiority of the masses, and naked fear of their growing prominence and power. Just as St. Clare becomes distinctly more religious in the Russian—indeed, an exaggeration (if such can be imagined) of Stowe's religiosity is a trait of many prerevolutionary versions—Alfred becomes even more arrogant, as shown most obviously in his proud denunciation of theology and his foolish claim (which might well be due to a creative mistranslation) that the "invention" of gunpowder demonstrates white superiority.

By this time, in short, we see a confident appropriation of *Uncle Tom's Cabin* by the educated elites not only for use in their projects of enlightenment but also as a theater for staging their own self-representation: where Khomyakov and Nikolai Turgenev had seen their own landowner class mirrored through St. Clare, Murakhina's St. Clare becomes a hero of uplift. That *Uncle Tom* also spins an entertaining yarn was no drawback, in this age of emergent mass culture; yet the novel in Russia clearly retained much of its status as a "classic"—in contrast to its contemporaneous US exploitation through sales of everything from tobacco and sugar to health food and brooms—no doubt in part because of its baptism by Tolstoy.[91] It was certainly a classic for Russian readers of all ages by 1917, going through more than fifty editions between 1880 and 1916, often in large print runs.

3

The Early Soviet Period (to 1945)

Tom closed his eyes, and shuddered at the dark, atheistic words.
Uncle Tom's Cabin

Legree, like most godless and cruel men, was superstitious.
Uncle Tom's Cabin

THE HISTORIAN SHEILA FITZPATRICK has described the central dynamic of early Soviet cultural politics as a struggle between the Bolshevik Party and the intelligentsia—"two great protagonists," she writes, that in many ways "had more in common than either cared to admit":

> [They] shared an idea of culture as something that (like revolution) an enlightened minority brought to the masses in order to uplift them. . . . What would now be called urban popular culture was condemned out of hand by the culture-bringers inside and outside the party as "vulgar," "trivial," and "petty-bourgeois" . . . , the last epithet being equally derogatory whether it came from the lips of a wellborn liberal intellectual or those of a militant proletarian Bolshevik. . . . [They shared] a highly developed sense of historical mission and moral superiority. The collective self-consciousness that created the Russian intelligentsia in the mid-nineteenth century was, above all, consciousness of a mission to enlighten, to serve the people, to act as critic and conscience of the state.[1]

Uncle Tom's Cabin does not fit easily into any one sector of a discursive/polemical field defined by a relatively liberal, crusading (sometimes religious) educated elite and a militant, illiberal, and antireligious Bolshevism. It is a religious book, and in that sense anathema to Bolsheviks (and to some on the other side as well); it is an "engaged" and politically consequential book, and in that sense exemplary for activists in both camps; it is a book that criticizes urban capitalist exploitation as well as plantation slavery, and thus again provisionally acceptable to many on both sides; it is an enormously popular book, and certainly too "vulgar" and "trivial" for many readers, Bolsheviks or not; it is (for some) a great book as well, constituting (in the judgment of the translator Murakhina) "an immortal trio" with *Robinson Crusoe* and *Don Quixote*.[2] So what is a new, revolutionary culture supposed to do with such a volatile, multivalent text?

To my knowledge, seven Soviet editions of *Uncle Tom's Cabin* appeared in the 1920s: two in 1925, three in 1928, one in 1930, and one other edition.[3] The period immediately preceding these editions—including the miseries of World War 1, the elation and disorder associated with the February and October Revolutions of 1917, and the terrible destruction of the Civil War (1918–21)—saw enormous suffering and catastrophic economic collapse, and it was not until around 1922 that the situation began to stabilize. Some publishing continued during the chaos, of course; in the midst of the war (in 1919) Maxim Gorky managed to found the first Soviet magazine for children, *Northern Lights*, though it ran for only a year—short lifespans were typical of journals in these times—and did not presage a post–Civil War boom in children's literature, which remained a deficit item until decade's end.[4] Major cultural changes were occurring, with the quest for sustenance leading to mass migrations from city to country (and, later, back again to the towns), tensions emerging between the party and the older educated elite (leading to the emigration of thousands and culminating with 160 liberal intellectuals being ejected from the country in 1922), and the beginnings of serious strife between the state and the church, especially after March 1922, when the money-starved government demanded that the church hand over precious metals and other treasures. Anticlerical waves came and went throughout the twenties but made a definitive return at the end of the decade with the beginnings of the First Five-Year Plan; "by the end of 1930," writes historian Ronald Suny, "four-fifths of all village churches were no longer operating."[5]

The period in which the seven main 1920s editions of Stowe's novel appeared—roughly 1922–30—was a period of unusually intense cultural experimentation, especially in comparison to the coming long repression that would find alleviation only after Joseph Stalin's death in 1953. If the decade's *Uncle Tom's Cabin* adaptations demonstrate remarkable imagination and well-nigh Constructivist formal abandon, they also perform their experiments on the text strictly in accord with Soviet ideology as it was then taking shape. They are *adaptations* in the fullest sense, going beyond any previous or later versions in the extent to which they reshape *Uncle Tom*; as we will see, that reshaping was executed on the basis of principles diametrically opposed to those in operation in (for example) the Murakhina versions. Although far less drastically altered editions began to reappear in the early 1940s, it turns out that no more or less complete translation of *Uncle Tom's Cabin* appeared in the Soviet Union until 1977.[6]

Some of the attitudes informing the 1920s revisions are revealed in the introduction to the book written by E. Vinogradskaia, whose name is attached to two of the adaptations:

> Stowe's book hit a sore spot and agitated sharply for the freeing of the Negroes. In truth, Stowe did not expose the root of the conflict but only appealed to the pity and sympathy of her readers. Nonetheless, the book did play its role. Kind slaveholders are described in it, and the author's sympathy for them is apparent—as though it were a matter of [individual] people, rather than in the existing government/state order, when Negroes are being bought and sold like goods and the law protects slaveholders. And what of the figure of Tom himself, delineated in the novel with love, the figure of a downtrodden Negro, who doesn't know how to answer blows with blows? This isn't the way the story would be written today. But the book is now eighty years old, and it continues to be read with great interest and continues to move and to touch. . . .
>
> In 1865 all American Negroes were declared free citizens but in fact still do not enjoy rights equal to those of whites.
>
> The bourgeoisie fights with all the means at its disposal against equality for Negroes, not shying away from violence and murder.
>
> Only in recent years has an organized movement of struggle against the bourgeoisie developed among Negroes. The Negro worker is looking for friends among the workers of America and the world.[7]

This brusque statement sets the tone for many prefaces to come. Stowe is portrayed as a "mere" (if still effective) sentimental moralist, without the analytic ability that subtler earlier readers like Chernyshevsky had discerned in her work. Remarkably, and in contrast to the majority of later forewords, the book's religiosity goes unmentioned, perhaps because alluding to it might have necessitated a more elaborate explanation of why the book was being published in the first place. The kind of criticism of the current American order introduced by Gorbunov-Posadov is granted central emphasis, along with an open call for an international socialist response to the problems of inequality. Most importantly, the model of *heroism* offered by Stowe—the pacifist Tom— is flatly judged to be out of date, even if Tom's story remains a "touching" one. The question of heroism becomes crucial at this point, if only because the (ideological) *value* of Tom needs to be rethought if, with the discrediting of Stowe's Christian horizon, he is reduced to being simply a courageous victim. And if Tom is not the hero of the story, then who is?

George Harris, of course: of the six editions I've seen from the 1920s, three end not with George Shelby's eulogy to Uncle Tom but with George Harris going to Africa (sometimes specifically Liberia) to work for "the liberation of [his] people."[8] This decision to culminate with George, and thus to close on a note of productive, self-conscious defiance, is unique to these early Soviet editions. It might not be going too far to say that these endings also point to wider anticolonial struggle (a long-standing Leninist preoccupation) as the relevant frame for reading the book within the contemporary—interestingly, the illustrations to the 1928 Vinogradskaia edition depict a weirdly "colonial African" world, replete with palm trees, planters wearing colonial-style helmets and khakis, and slaves in loose gowns, rather than the rural American garb and landscape familiar from most other versions. In the same edition, in a section equivalent to the "Middle Passage" chapter, the wise "young man" on the train who reproaches the "stranger" (i.e., the man who has just been discussing slavery with Simon Legree) for his sentimental naïveté is turned into a "foreigner," suggesting that the book is again being situated within a framework of international and geopolitical concerns rather than merely local or ethical/metaphysical ones.[9]

A more puzzling related feature of these early editions is their tendency to omit Stowe's comparisons of slavery with capitalist exploitation (particularly in "Miss Ophelia's Experiences, Continued"), passages that would seem wholly consonant with a leftist viewpoint. It is indeed difficult to determine the reasons for these cuts. On the one hand, it may be that *Uncle Tom's Cabin* was already emerging as a distinctly anti-American (rather than anticapitalist) book, so Stowe's more radical social diagnoses might have seemed to contradict this function and muddy the ideological waters. On the other hand, and perhaps more probably, these early editions are definitely oriented toward children, and therefore (like other, earlier children's versions) tend to pare down or eliminate entirely Stowe's passages of political dialectic. The distinction between "censorship" and "adaptation for children" becomes a very blurry one in such cases. At any rate, the majority of later editions (and all the major post–World War 2 ones) retain these sections even when children are the intended audience.

In spite of George's prominence, Tom is certainly not discarded in these editions. His image, however, undergoes a clear if subtle secularization. He is changed, without too much difficulty, from a very religious man into a very *moral* man:

Uncle Tom was a sort of patriarch in religious matters, in the neighborhood. Having, naturally, an organization in which the *morale* was strongly predominant, together with a greater breadth and cultivation of mind than obtained among his companions, he was looked up to with great respect, as a sort of minister among them; and the simple, hearty, sincere style of his exhortations might have edified even better educated persons. But it was in prayer that he especially excelled. (Stowe, 35)

In matters of morality Uncle Tom enjoyed a special authority. Deeply moral by nature and having a mind both clearer and more capable of being educated than those of the majority of his fellow tribesmen, he involuntarily distinguished himself from the people around him, who readily acknowledged his superiority over them and looked upon him as one of the very best of people. And indeed, his simple, heartfelt convictions, shot through with sincere feeling, would have been able to touch more cultured people as well.[10] (Leonti'eva translation)

The condescension of Stowe's description is if anything intensified in the Leonti'eva, particularly in the assertion that Tom was actually "more *capable* of being educated" than most of his "fellow tribesmen." The important thing, though, is that Tom's strength is of conviction and character rather than of faith; at his death as represented in the 1925 Vinogradskaia version, Tom states not that "the Lord Jesus" has given him victory (Stowe, 426), but simply (and "with unusual conviction") "'I endured . . . I have conquered.'"[11] Indeed, in the Leonti'eva version Tom shows signs of advancing entirely beyond religious superstition, and his "simple, heartfelt convictions" now derive in part from a mysterious, unidentified secular source:

Because Tom was "literate"—that is, read haltingly, syllable by syllable—
he often invited his Negro comrades over to his cabin. There he read to
them aloud from a book that spoke about nature, about heavenly bodies,
about remarkable people and great fighters for freedom. The Negroes
listened to his reading with pleasure.[12]

This is a pretty crude adjustment, of course, and more sophisticated
and informed readers may well have been able to identify the real
"book" hidden between the lines. Other changes, which involve the
representation of character in the novel, are not only subtler but reflect
cultural shifts occurring between 1925 and 1928 as well.

Most interesting, perhaps, are the portrayals of Eva's death in the
two Vinogradskaia versions:

"O, God, this is dreadful!" [St. Clare] said, turning away in agony, and wringing Tom's hand, scarce conscious what he was doing. "O, Tom, my boy, it is killing me!"

Tom had his master's hands between his own; and, with tears streaming down his dark cheeks, looked up for help where he had always been used to look.

"Pray that this may be cut short!" said St. Clare,—"this wrings my heart."

"O, bless the Lord! it's over,—it's over, dear Master!" said Tom; "look at her."

The child lay panting on her pillows, as one exhausted,—the large clear eyes rolled up and fixed. Ah, what said those eyes, that spoke so much of heaven? Earth was past, and earthly pain; but so solemn, so mysterious, was the triumphant brightness of that face, that it checked even the sobs of sorrow. They pressed around her, in breathless stillness.

"Eva," said St. Clare, gently.

In terrible torment, almost unconsciously, St. Clare seized Tom by the hand.

"Tom, my friend!"

Tom took his master's hand into his own. Hot tears ran down his black cheeks.

"Look, master," he said.

The eyes of the little girl opened, and she gazed steadily ahead.

"Eva!" cried St. Clare again. "Eva!"

A joyful smile lit up her little face. She sighed deeply—and all was over.

"Goodbye, dear child! Never again will we see your gentle little face."[13]

Cont. p. 68

She did not hear.

"O, Eva, tell us what you see! What is it?" said her father.

A bright, a glorious smile passed over her face, and she said, brokenly,—"O! love,—joy,—peace!" gave one sigh, and passed from death unto life!

"Farewell, beloved child! the bright, eternal doors have closed after thee; we shall see thy sweet face no more." (Stowe, 304)

The religious trappings are gone, of course, although much of the "sentimental tableau" quality is retained, both here and elsewhere in the early Soviet editions. In the 1928 version by the same editor, however, the first two-and-a-half lines (from "In terrible torment" to "his own") are cut, replaced by the simple phrase: "Tom looked at Eva, his gaze never leaving her."[14] In other words, the crucial moment of spiritual connection between master and slave at the point of crisis—that experience that links them in a common (sentimental) humanity—is eradicated. The possibilities of communion across racial/class lines are reconfigured, with Tom ultimately connected to the suffering, helpless child alone. This new emphasis on nonreconciliation (while still siphoning off some sentiment) is reflected in the same edition's foregrounding of Aunt Chloe (particularly her reactions to Tom's sale and death) and the complete removal of Topsy, the central exhibit, in her relation to Miss Ophelia, of the coming-together-of-opposites in the novel.

The greatest exception to the George Harris–centered adaptations is certainly Alexander Deich's 1928 version, another edition intended for young audiences and probably the most sensitive Russian reworking of the novel to appear in the 1920s. Deich (1893–1972) was an important theater critic and all-round presence on the cultural scene from the 1920s onward; an experienced translator as well, he clearly made an attempt in his condensation-adaptation to remain faithful to Stowe's original vision. Deich not only retains the "novel-of-ideas" side of *Uncle Tom*—the debates between St. Clare and Ophelia, for instance—but stresses the novel's testimonies of suffering, such as those of Prue, Hagar, and Cassy. Indeed, the problem of how to maintain hope under conditions of oppression, of whether suffering has any positive value— a problem that, for many Soviet readers of the 1920s, would have been pressing indeed—becomes the central theme of the Deich adaptation, which elides the active resisters George and Eliza entirely. When Cassy, a "demon [or] angel of vengeance," tempts Tom to kill Legree, Deich offers an ethical précis of his hero's predicament: "How to preserve a joyous faith in the final triumph of justice with a head ever bent below the yoke, and a heart burning at offenses given not only to one's self, but to others still weaker?"[15] Although Tom's death at the hands of Legree prompts Deich's George Shelby to dedicate his life to the abolitionist cause, this version maintains a genuine ambiguity right through to the end: Tom's firmness of principle and radical pacifism are honored (as is his physical beauty), even as Cassy's more violent proposals for escaping oppression are never finally invalidated. One can see how Deich's adaptation might have elicited actual ethical debate, rather than simply imparting a relatively monophonic lesson.

To be sure, Deich, like other adaptors, squeezes the religion out of the novel, mainly by translating Christian sentiment into ethical/ collective feeling. In Vinogradskaia's 1928 version, for instance, Tom remains with the other slaves (instead of going with Cassy) not because "the Lord's given [him] a work" (Stowe, 205) but because "my comrades need me."[16] Thus Tom can remain a sentimental hero without being a *religious* one. Stowe's religious frame is subjected to critique as well as elision, however, as can be seen in this remarkable revision of "An Evening in Uncle Tom's Cabin":

The room was soon filled with a motley assemblage, from the old gray-headed patriarch of eighty, to the young girl and lad of fifteen. A little harmless gossip ensued on various themes. . . . A few of the worshippers belonged to families hard by, who had got permission to attend, and who brought in various choice scraps of information, about the sayings and doings at the house and on the place, which circulated as freely as the same sort of small change does in higher circles.

After a while the singing commenced, to the evident delight of all present. Not even all the disadvantage

The Negroes gathered together and talked about domestic news, gossiped, as is the custom, and a bit later began singing. Their voices, naturally beautiful, sounded wild and passionate. The Negroes sang religious songs, and put all of their longing for liberation into them. They knew no true songs of freedom. The masters and the clergymen had taught them religious songs that spoke about liberation after death, in heaven. The unhappy, deceived people sang those fairy tales about "Jordan's shores," consoling themselves with hope for a better life after death.[17]

Cont. p. 70

of nasal intonation could prevent the effect of the naturally fine voices, in airs at once wild and spirited. The words were sometimes the well-known and common hymns sung in the churches about, and sometimes of a wilder, more indefinite character, picked up at camp-meetings. . . .

[Some of the songs] made incessant mention of "Jordan's banks," and "Canaan's fields," and the "New Jerusalem;" for the negro mind, impassioned and imaginative, always attaches itself in hymns and expressions of a vivid and pictorial nature; and, as they sung, some laughed, and some cried, and some clapped hands, or shook hands rejoicingly with each other, as if they had fairly gained the other side of the river. (Stowe, 34)

Stowe's characteristic mix of condescension, sympathy, and admiration is replaced by a more unambiguous "enlightened" pity, as well as another demystifying reinterpretation of religious desire in terms of a rather different kind of yearning. In a way, the observation that the slaves "knew no true songs of freedom" recalls Gorbunov-Posadov's comments on the hopeless superstitions of African religion—a classically elite sense of superiority persists, though translated into a different register. That is to say: the mechanism in Stowe's Christian worldview that enables such surprising reversals—the way the weak can become the strong, and the strong the weak—is removed, with both strong and weak now in clearly demarcated, earthbound positions. The weak can become strong only through secular effort: through education, organization, conscious resistance.

In the same vein, the powerful dialogue between Cassy and Tom in "The Quadroon's Story" becomes the occasion (in the Leonti'eva version) for both an intensification of Cassy's anguished skepticism and a strengthening of her character. Rather than simply speaking "with a wild, passionate utterance" (Stowe, 375), the Soviet Cassy tells the story of her sufferings and her doubts as part of a conscious, concealed effort to undermine Tom's faith; she guessed "precisely what was going on in Tom's soul, and [wanted] to disturb him even more."[18]

Squarely associating the consolations of "the sisters of the convent" with those who think "nothing [of] what our children suffer" (Stowe, 375), Leonti'eva's Cassy transmutes her passionate despair into a ringing argument—unanswered by Tom—against religious assurances:

> Do you really imagine that it's sufficient to give a person deceptive hope for some reward beyond the grave, that he won't feel the blows raining down on him from all sides, or that he might accept them with an obedient smile? . . . No, no, that's all lies, stupidity, and hypocrisy. . . . If there is a God, wouldn't it be better if he didn't let all the evil and injustice happen, rather than judge later something that he already allowed to occur?[19]

Again, Cassy's story is presented in this Soviet version as both passionately sincere and consciously stage-managed: when Tom becomes "frightened" by her "fire of madness," she notices his reaction and, calming herself "with fearful strength of will" (p. 217),[20] assures him he has nothing to fear from her, brings him a drink, and cuts him off even before the utterly nonplussed Tom has a chance to express his preference for "living water" (Stowe, 376). (Indeed, we might say that the great scene of Cassy's theatrical deception of Legree is here extended to her treatment of Tom as well!) We never see Tom convert to atheism, of course, but his religious exhortations virtually disappear from the text, and Cassy remains irreligious to the end. The whole conversation resembles a "scene of instruction," and seems to provide a model for the kind of dialogue that an anticlerical activist might have with a religious hanger-on: that is, for the work of propaganda (as opposed to agitation) in that word's strictest sense.[21] More generally, what this adaptation shows is how moments of crisis in Stowe's text can be developed in ways that, while certainly distorting the original, also expose certain tensions latent within it: the Communist Cassy is a plausible extension of her prototype.

But although *Uncle Tom's Cabin* showed itself to be fairly susceptible to Bolshevik modifications, it seems that the novel was still felt to be out of step with (in Katerina Clark's words) "the radical mood and industrial orientation of the Five-Year Plan period [1928–33]."[22] The 1930 adaptation by N. Moguchij was apparently the last printed edition to appear until 1941, with Stowe's voice falling largely silent in Russia during the Stalinist 1930s, the tumultuous and terrible years of industrialization, proletarian promotion, collectivization, and the great purges. As for the years between 1852 and 1857–58, we have no official record of a ban; however, one important text, the *Literary Encyclopedia* of 1930 (but written/compiled a couple of years earlier), may reflect something like a shift in authoritative opinion.

The *Encyclopedia*'s article on Stowe, included within a larger section on nineteenth-century American writers, compliments her on foreseeing "the preservation of actual slavery after its formal abolition" and for the "germs of sound social analysis" in her representation, but condemns her "attempt to reconcile the slaves with the masters in a religious sense" (p. 502).[23] The article concludes on a note of censorious finality:

> Although Soviet publishers have published Stowe's book, it is doubtful that it should be recognized as desirable [reading] for Soviet youth. The strength of her realistic representation of slavery is neutralized by the religious resolution of the conflict; her characters are mere sketches; in tone and tempo, the novel falls outside the style of our epoch.[24]

Apart from all the religion in the book—doubtless the main reason for its failure to be published in the 1930s—what else about *Uncle Tom's Cabin* "[fell] outside of the style of [that] epoch?" To be sure, the book's generic and ideological instability was a problem, particularly in a context where the state was bent on not only monopolizing production but also imposing a "single social ethos" on reading practice as such.[25] The novel's racism possibly, though not necessarily, presented another challenge (this was, among other things, the period of the "pilgrimages" of black Communists and fellow-travelers to the USSR), and perhaps the book's proximity to the "peasant" theme generated nervousness (collectivized peasants sometimes referred to the new rural order as a "second serfdom," with good reason).[26] But I would guess that the central character of Tom posed the greatest difficulties of ideological assimilation.

As Clark has shown, the value of heroic self-sacrifice—for the sake of the great project of building socialism, for the party, even for "History"— was of crucial importance for the culture that developed in the early Soviet period and in part represented a continuation (and transformation) of earlier intelligentsia valorizations of martyrdom for the "cause."[27] Yet Tom's martyrdom differs from this model, and in several ways. He doesn't die fighting but rather dies (precisely) *not* fighting, in a mode of resistance profoundly at odds with the iron ethos of the time of shock labor and socialist competition. Years later in her book on *Uncle Tom's Cabin* (1975), and writing well after Stalinist models of heroism had become passé, Raisa Orlova would subtly allude to this aspect of

Stowe, praising it in a way that both critiques masculinist heroics and harmonizes with American discussions of the book's *gendering* of activism:

> Stowe's book . . . admonished and summoned readers to abolish an injustice that had endured for centuries. Her summons, moreover, was uttered gently, in a womanly, a Christian way, virtually with humility, directed to those who owned slaves.[28]

Then there is the question of Tom's intransigence vis-à-vis "the world." Although Stowe obviously instrumentalizes his death for the cause of abolition, Tom does not himself die on behalf of any earthly cause. He dies for his Christian-pacifist beliefs, which crucially require his *disobedience* to worldly authority (Legree), rather than functioning as its tool. In a society increasingly characterized by ruthless top-down administration and centralization of power, such a stance becomes subversive, and may (unconsciously) have been perceived as such by the Soviet cultural decision makers. Again, Orlova—herself a dissident from the mid-1960s onward—identifies this tension when she faults those American writers who mock passive "Uncle Tomism" for missing the real point. Simply to associate Tom with advocates of reformist, gradualist solutions to America's racial problems, she writes, is to forget the essence of his resistance—"the fact that Tom refused to beat the Negro woman, that he refused to fulfill his master's order, that he went to death for the sake of his convictions."[29] Perhaps it would not be wrong to suggest that this particular positive aspect of Stowe's representation might have been more obvious, and more important, to a Soviet observer of the 1970s than to her counterpart in the United States.[30] In a famous poem written right around the time she was reading *Uncle Tom's Cabin* (1938), Marina Tsvetaeva expresses the core of this negative revolt, in lines that I would choose to read as (partially) a tribute to Tom, whose image was fresh in the poet's mind:

I refuse to be. In
The madhouse of the inhuman
I refuse to live.
With the wolves of the market place

I refuse to howl.
Among the sharks of the plain
I refuse to swim down
where moving backs make a current.

I have no need of holes
for ears, nor prophetic eyes:
to your mad world there is
one answer: to refuse![31]

So although Tom has the Higher Goal constantly in mind, his is
an ethic intensely hostile to any sort of expedience and judges each
act (rather than the cumulative outcome) in relation to that absolute
standard—no Pascalian wagers allowed here! Considered on its own
terms, Tom's death contains an incalculable element of excess that
looks simply nonsensical (absurdly passive or even self-destructive)
from the point of view of any "plan."[32] (This points, I think, to an important aspect of Stowe's genius: Tom's death seems uncomfortably close
to senseless, lonely suffering, and part of the book's "sentimental
power"—and perhaps its offensiveness as well—results from the never-
resolved strain of her attempt to absorb that pain into a providential
narrative.) If one argues, on the other hand, that Soviet ideals of sacrifice
are themselves residually religious, then another problem emerges—for
Tom's death, explicitly saturated in Christian mythology, reveals the
hidden metaphysics of the ideal of sacrifice just a bit too clearly and
paradoxically works as a kind of demystification by reflection.

The main exception to the Soviet *Tom* ban of the 1930s was evidently
the stage version created by Alexandra Brushtein (1884–1968), an important Soviet dramatist and prose writer. Born in Vilnius into a Jewish
family well known in the city and beyond—her physician father, Iakov
Vygodsky (Jakub Wygodzki, 1857–1941), was distinguished in medicine,
politics, and prose writing (mainly in Yiddish)—and educated in St.
Petersburg, Brushtein became involved in theater during the Russian
Civil War (1918–21). In 1922, director Alexander Briantsev took her on as
a member of his fledgling Theater of the Young Spectator in Petrograd
(later Leningrad; this was the first Soviet children's theater), and for
this and other theaters she produced many original plays and theatrical
adaptations right into the 1960s, largely with children's audiences in
mind.[33] Between 1927 and 1966, Brushtein wrote or cowrote at least
four different versions of *Uncle Tom's Cabin*, all of which became well
known almost exclusively through their staged versions (none were
distributed widely in published form), performed from 1927 through at
least the 1960s.[34] Although at least one other Soviet author adapted
Uncle Tom's Cabin for the stage—prose writer Vladimir Lidin, for the

Figure 5. Photograph of the 1928 production of the Alexandra Brushtein–Boris Zon adaptation of *Uncle Tom's Cabin*, directed by Zon with sets by V. I. Bejer, taken at the State Theater of the Young Spectator. Photograph courtesy of Laurence Senelick.

Moscow Art Theater in 1926—Brushtein created by far the most substantial and popular Soviet theatrical reworkings of the novel.[35]

The 1927–28 Leningrad production at the Theater of the Young Spectator was by all accounts a popular one (fig. 5), not least because of director and co-adaptor Boris Zon's decision to bring the audience close to the action: as they passed, actors playing slave traders and other evildoers were frequently pummeled by youthful audience members whipped into a frenzy by their villainy.[36] An effective, Negro spiritual-influenced score by composer Nikolai Strel'nikov (1888–1939; later one of the founders of the Soviet operetta tradition) had actors, choir, and audience members rocking back and forth, especially during a number called "The Ohio River Weeps."[37]

Ten years later, in the midst of the Stalinist terror, the play was readapted by Brushtein and Zon for an adult audience under the title *Black Merchandise* (but evidently often staged simply as *Uncle Tom's Cabin*). This highly dramatic, fluent, and action-centered adaptation removes (yet again) the entire New Orleans–St. Clare narrative, with all its discussion and debate. Aspects of both George Shelby and Little Eva are folded into "Dora," the daughter (rather than the son) of the Shelbys; Tom, Eliza, and Topsy (now the daughter of George and Eliza!) are sold to "Jerry" (i.e., Simon Legree); and Eliza contrives the escape of all three through the theatrically sensational "ghost" ruse concocted by Cassy in the novel. Even Tom comes to learn the necessity of strong action, and Jerry-Legree is left alone onstage at the end to lament:

> JERRY: The ground, the ground is shifting beneath my feet! Negroes, who hadn't dared to peep in my direction, whom I had in the palm of my hand, are shaking their fists at me? And Tom—he was praying morning to night. What is happening? Could it really be . . . the end?
> [*Curtain*][38]

The play contains plenty of theatrically effective personae and moments, including a broadly comic, minstrelesque Aunt Chloe (who dances with Tom across the stage) and a cruel scene where Jerry's daughter Fanny torments a starving Topsy:

> FANNY: OK, let's play—you be the dog and obey me . . . (*She lifts a bun up in the air.*)
> TOPSY: I don't know how . . .
> FANNY: Oh, you! You stand like this, like you were a dog, and obey me sitting on your hind legs. (*Shows her how to do this.*) Well?
> (*Topsy stands up.*)
> FANNY: (handing her the bun) Here!
> (*Topsy extends her hand.*)
> FANNY: What kind of dog are you, if you grab it with your hand! No, use your teeth!
> (*Topsy tries to seize the bun with her teeth.*)
> FANNY: (teasing her as she would a little dog) Bite! Bite! Bite! Grrr, grrr.[39]

These and other bits of "business" were evidently retained in the later Brushtein adaptations as well and no doubt came to be expected by audiences.[40]

The quite entertaining adaptation—probably the most explicitly anti-Fascist Russian-language reworking of *Tom*—enjoyed considerable popularity and was put on by theater companies all over the Soviet Union. The program notes from a 1938 Krasnoyarsk production give a good sense of the ideological framework within which Stalin-era cultural authorities hoped the play would be received:

[In selecting *Uncle Tom's Cabin* and] in showing the full horror of slavery, the greatest form of the oppression of one person by another, the theater wishes to remind the Soviet spectator of the cruel oppression and injustice to which the Negroes of America, the peoples of colonial nations, and nations beaten down by fascism are subject. For to this day, Negroes are not regarded as humans in America: they do not have the right to live in the same areas of cities as do whites, to ride with them in the same tram and railway cars; they even have special floors set apart for them in prisons.

Today in America a law of impunity for participants in lynching of blacks is being discussed.

It is impossible to imagine anything more savage, more barbaric. The condition in India, in Abyssinia, in all colonial or in so-called "mandated" territories differs little from the condition of Negroes under slavery. Attempting to finally make Negroes obedient, to destroy their longing for freedom, slaveholders used the tried and true weapon of *religion*.

The church taught Negroes (like Tom) obedience, blind submission to their owners, and promised a heavenly kingdom as reward for the torments and oppression on earth. But the opiate of religion could not destroy their striving for freedom; they rose up and struggled and could not come to terms with oppression and injustice, or being treated like two-legged livestock (George). . . .

Living in a happy country, in the country of socialism, we must recall the cruel oppression of our foreign brothers and not forget Stalin's words: "We must move forward so that the working class of the entire world, looking at us, might say—there it is, my front line, there it is, my shock brigade, there it is, my workers' state, there it is, my fatherland."[41]

As we will soon see, this discourse—all of it justified vis-à-vis racism in the United States, contemporary colonialism, and fascism, and all of it ironic vis-à-vis the murderous state-driven terror lashing the USSR in 1938—would return to surround *Tom* adaptations during the "high Cold War" period of the late forties–early fifties.[42] In the meantime, however, if *Uncle Tom's Cabin* was staged in the USSR during the immediately succeeding years (1939–41), its presentation must have been framed in different terms, given the pact reached with German fascism in 1939, and (later) the Union's entry into World War 2 as an ally of the United States.

Indeed, *Uncle Tom*-the-Book reappeared in early 1941—six months before the war would begin—under the editorial auspices of the remarkable Kornei Chukovsky (1882–1969), a distinguished literary scholar, essayist, translator, and author of highly popular and imaginative works in verse and prose for children. Chukovsky had published important translations of and commentaries on Walt Whitman (the "poet-anarchist," in Chukovsky's phrase) among others before the revolution, and in his own person constituted a historical link between the pre-revolutionary, liberal educated elite and the Soviet cultural order, the latter pretty much fully formed by 1941.[43]

Chukovsky had headed up the Anglo-American division of the World Literature publishing house since 1918, and perhaps he suggested to the relatively new *Children's Literature* (a house founded in 1933) that it might be time to bring back Stowe's novel, given the recent publication of the then-Communist Richard Wright's 1938 story collection *Uncle Tom's Children* in Russian translation (1939) and the imminent appearance of the same author's *Native Son* (1940) in Russian. Indeed, the Soviet cultural press contrasted Stowe and Wright at the time, suggesting that *Uncle Tom's Cabin* had been recovered at a moment when Communist African American writers had both returned to the traditions of the protest novel and begun to formulate critiques of those traditions. Interestingly, one reviewer of the Chukovsky translation both compared Stowe's novel to Wright's collection and claimed, falsely, that this was the first Soviet appearance of *Uncle Tom's Cabin* ("the religious attitudes that penetrate several chapters of the novella [sic] were hitherto felt to be impenetrable obstacles to publication").[44] Inasmuch as the tandem publication of Wright's books alongside Stowe's can be regarded as a signal example of the USSR's participation in the construction of a "world literature" in the 1930s–1940s, it seems that this participation had amnesia vis-à-vis the 1920s—the pre-Stalinist cultural order, which had its own international dimension—as a precondition.[45]

Certainly, the translation (actually carried out by Chukovsky's son Nikolai and daughter-in-law Marina) is considerably more complete, and far gentler in its revisions, than any of the 1920s versions. Some of the religion remains (such as in the "Evening in Uncle Tom's Cabin" chapter, where the devotion of the slaves is shown basically as Stowe presents it), and the book ends not with George Harris but with George Shelby's eulogy to Tom—although he exhorts the former slaves not to "be as honest and faithful and Christian as [Tom] was" (Stowe, 447), but rather only to "think of [their] freedom" (a phrase also in Stowe) each time they pass by the cabin.[46]

Rather than inserting commentary (as Vinogradskaia sometimes does) or modifying the text (as Leonti'eva does), the Chukovskys tend to rely on cuts in order to de-Christianize the book's texture, as at the end of "The Quadroon's Story," where Tom's religious encouragements are simply removed (without Cassy being converted into a well-nigh

conscious atheist as in the Leonti'eva version). The scene of Tom's death—
obviously a crucial moment for any translator—is simply shortened by
adding an ellipsis space and eliminating all text from the point where
Legree "[smites] his victim to the ground" (Stowe, 421) until the shaken
Sambo declares that Tom is "most gone" (Stowe, 422). There is a very
substantial elision, however, in "Miss Ophelia's Experiences, Continued," where St. Clare's entire comparison of himself with his brother,
Alfred, his references to capitalism, and his prophecy of a *dies irae* are
removed.[47] Once again, the reasons for the cut are hard to pin down: it
might have been a matter of space (but why not cut other sections?), or
a matter of making the book more child friendly (but then why include
the more abstruse material about Louis XVI, Pius IX, and sansculottes
in "Henrique"?) or a matter of the content (but *what*, exactly, was
problematic)?

The preface by Kornei Chukovsky is more interesting than the translation itself, primarily because he found occasion to reflect on it late
in life when preparing his *Collected Works*. Unlike the vast majority
of Soviet prefacers, Chukovsky finds much to praise from a literary
point of view in Stowe's work. He compares her at length to the great
nineteenth-century Russian writers, in particular to Gogol (in her use of
satire and broad caricature), Turgenev, and his favorite poet and early
Stowe editor Nikolai Nekrasov. Chukovsky points especially to how
Stowe's representation of planter "aristocracy" resonates with the Russian counterparts—an observation that recalls, unconsciously of course,
the early responses of Engel'son, Nikolai Turgenev, and Khomyakov.
Her great "strength of portraiture," he writes, gives her characters—he
singles out Adolph, Topsy, Marks, the St. Clares, Mr. Shelby, Little Eva,
Aunt Chloe, and especially Miss Ophelia—the quality of life. In figures
like St. Clare, Stowe shows her mastery of a characterization so "rich in
contradictory nuances that it cannot fit into any verbal formula."[48]

He is less enthusiastic about Tom, however, whom he calls "the
least attractive thing in the book." And yet, because of Stowe's "huge,
realistic . . . talent," she manages to show, precisely through Tom,
"something entirely different" from what she wanted to show. Making
use of socialist realist cliché, Chukovsky claims that a "true" realist can
never "alter or distort reality for the purposes of propagandizing his
mistaken opinions."[49]

[Stowe] wanted to praise religion as the faithful support for millions of
black-skinned people, but showed—contrary to her own intentions—the
terrible role that religion played in their lives, how it prevents their

freedom, their struggle with their inhuman owners, and how useful religion is to all planters, all slaveholders, all the Legrees and Haleys of the world. For had Tom not been seduced from childhood with the temptations of happiness beyond the grave, he would, with his mind and physical strength, his nobility and manliness, immediately have organized an uprising of Negroes and would have won freedom for himself and for them.[50]

One can see Chukovsky's point, but this remains a clumsy remark, informed by a singularly undialectical sense of Stowe's way of using religion, and seems at odds with Chukovsky's fine appreciation of the contradictions inherent in the portrayals of St. Clare and Miss Ophelia. And indeed, it turns out that Chukovsky was himself deeply dissatisfied with the article, as revealed by a diary entry from 1966, when he was both in the hospital recovering from pneumonia (he was to die only three years later) and looking over the proofs for his *Works*:

> 25 March. It's already my tenth day in hospital. . . . I'm undergoing terrible psychological torment. Just now, holding the proofs for the third volume [of the *Collected Works*], I read my article about Stowe. Shameful, banal, lisping, fakery. If, when I was young and fighting for new forms for the critical article, someone had shown me that piece, written in Stalinist days for Detgiz [the State Children's Publishing House] (and Detgiz rejected it, as they were struggling against "Chukovsky-ism" at the time)—if I'd been shown that flaccid, bloodless little article, I would have burst into tears of grief. I devoted my whole life so that such hypocritical, facile little essays wouldn't exist on earth—and here in my *Collected Works* this moldy article, lacking any spark of Chukovsky-ism, is offered up to readers as a model.[51]

The term "Chukovsky-ism" is shorthand for the kind of playful, quasi-absurdist, Lewis-Carroll–like children's poetry of which Chukovsky, in his youth an associate of many experimental poets, was a master—this, in contrast to the official socialist-realist and "revolutionary romanticist" dogma with which his article is unhappily saturated. What Chukovsky's renunciation suggests, however, is that *Uncle Tom's Cabin* may have been revived as a children's book precisely as a "realist" alternative to "Chukovsky-ism" (the latter a mode practiced by other major writers as well, such as Samuil Marshak). Certainly, the book would prove a handy instrument for propagating official doctrines on reality, as the next phase of its reception shows.

4

Uncle Tom, Cold Warrior

They were always abusing each other's opinions and practices, and yet never a whit the less absorbed in each other's society; in fact, the very contrariety seemed to unite them, like the attraction between opposite poles of the magnet.

Uncle Tom's Cabin (on St. Clare and his brother, Alfred)

KORNEI CHUKOVSKY may not have even known about the edition of the 1941 translation (together with his preface, much altered) published in Sverdlovsk in 1950. It is safe to say that he would not have been pleased. The original preface contained a good deal about Stowe's early life, but the later edition removes virtually all that material, except the references to her poverty, and all of Chukovsky's comparisons of Stowe's novel with Russian literature are cut. Added are five paragraphs of a more political nature, focused entirely on the contemporary American situation. Chukovsky had concluded his original essay with entirely accurate remarks on the postemancipation discrimination against and systemic exploitation of blacks in the United States. The newly augmented preface adds mention of lynching and the activities of the Klan and white supremacists—but then it goes considerably further:

> Especially today, when the United States is at such high speed becoming the nation of fascism, the life of "free" blacks has become heavy and tormenting, so that even the epoch of slavery might seem happier to them. The kindling of racial hatred has reached unheard-of dimensions in Truman's imperialist America, dimensions that Stowe could not have foreseen. . . . Contemporary America, under the power of the smart

operators of Wall Street, the America that has instigated a new war, has
spawned a fascistic, barbaric relationship to blacks. The most nightmarish
pages from the past, as described by Stowe, pale in comparison to the
sufferings undergone right now by the great-grandchildren of Uncle
Tom.[1]

One need not, I think, be an apologist for the American racial order to
find these comments a tad hyperbolic. With the onset of the Cold War
in 1946 (after a brief period of warm Soviet-American relations during
the war), anti–United States rhetoric became one of the expected features
of any preface to *Uncle Tom's Cabin*, although the language became
progressively less shrill over time.[2]

A grim and revealing example of the uses made of Stowe under
conditions of late-Stalinist hysteria appeared in a 1949 adaptation of the
book by V. S. Val'dman.[3] Although more full than the 1920s editions,
this version marks something of a return to those more uninhibited reworkings: instead of the book ending with Shelby exhorting the former
slaves to remember their freedom and "honest" Uncle Tom, readers are
exhorted to struggle (in capital letters) "for freedom and equality
throughout the world." Its afterword was written by Efim Grigorievich
Etkind (1918–99), at that time a young professor in Leningrad and later
famous both as a superb scholar of French literature and as a dissident
who in 1974 had to leave the USSR permanently after being removed
from his teaching post. What is surprising, given Etkind's later work,
is the monotonic sloganeering of the afterword. It has none of the
literary-critical spark of Chukovsky's introduction—that author's later
renunciation notwithstanding—and consists essentially of sentences
like these: "[Negroes] are just as lacking in rights as they were one
hundred years ago when Stowe wrote her book. . . . The history of
American capitalism is the most terrible, most shameful chapter in the
history of bourgeois society. 'On every dollar are traces of blood,' wrote
V. I. Lenin in his famous 'Letter to American Workers.'"[4] I suspect that
an explanation for this afterword might be on hand in Etkind's later
autobiographical work, *Notes of a Non-Conspirator*, where he describes
how already in the late 1940s—during a time of intense, growing, and
officially promoted antagonism toward Jews (labeled with the code
word "rootless cosmopolitans") in the USSR—he had undergone a
prorabótka, or public "working over." This amounted to (in his words)
"the 'correction' of an individual personality by the group . . . , a meeting
set up in advance at which an individual is exposed and criticized by a

series of speakers."[5] It happened right around the time his afterword to Stowe appeared:

> This was in 1949, when I was being accused of cosmopolitanism and anti-patriotism in the Leningrad Institute of Foreign Languages. One of my loyal colleagues had denounced me because in a lecture on "The Story of a Real Man" by [Soviet writer] Boris Polevoi . . . I had referred to Jack London's story "Love of Life" as a model for Polevoi. The zealous speakers assured a shocked and silent audience of teachers and students that Etkind disparaged and slandered Soviet literature, seeing in Soviet writers pitiful imitators of Western bourgeois authors, that he prostrated himself to the West, licked its boots, etc. I in my innocence insisted that Jack London was not at all a bourgeois writer, but rather an anti-bourgeois one, and that I had not presented Polevoi as an imitator but merely drawn a legitimate thematic parallel. I did not yet understand that no arguments could save me, since my fate had been decided in advance and my crime, like that of the other cosmopolitans, lay not in anything I had said but in the fact that I was a Jew.[6]

It is difficult to know whether this *prorabótka* occurred just before or after the afterword was written; however, it seems reasonable to surmise that Etkind may have taken the opportunity openly to demonstrate the proper attitude toward "the West" by writing a preface to a book— Stowe's—that might be used without strain as an occasion for embarking on severe criticism of the United States, thereby emitting the correct patriotic signals. This is only a guess, of course, but there can be no doubt that the stakes were very high indeed for Etkind, beyond even the usual professional ones (he was removed from his teaching post in Leningrad and had to relocate to a pedagogical institute in Tula, south of Moscow): the late 1940s–early 1950s were marked by severe repression (with high-ranking and professional Jews a specially targeted group), and "the [estimated] total number of prisoners in labor camps and colonies rose from 1,460,676 in 1945 to 2,468,524 in 1953."[7]

Of the many ironies attendant upon the Russian and Soviet reception of *Uncle Tom's Cabin*, the novel's role in this drama of crippling ideological and physical coercion is perhaps the most painful. To be sure, some Soviet writers in the post–World War 2 period, when dealing with Stowe's novel as prefacers or otherwise, took the opportunity to make justified criticisms of conditions in the United States; the same Boris Polevoi mentioned by Etkind wrote an often-reprinted preface in which he describes the persecution and marginalization of Paul Robeson as an example of ongoing racism.[8] Doubtless there were others (and not those in Etkind's precarious position) who took merely cynical advantage of Stowe in order to fashion (through the inevitable contrast with the American situation) maudlin panegyrics to the Soviet nation. A good example would be a verse titled "Uncle Tom's Cabin," penned in the 1950s or 1960s by Sergei Mikhalkov, author of the lyrics to the Soviet national anthem (recently revived by Vladimir Putin) and justly described as "Stalin's poet laureate."[9] Mikhalkov describes a theatrical staging of Stowe's novel during which (in a scene depicting the "Slave Warehouse") a little girl in the audience was so moved that she apparently walked onstage and offered money to one of the actors in order to buy the "slaves'" freedom—Little Eva in the flesh:

She was silent and waited,
And this was the moment
When, in an impulse countering Evil,
Good was more powerful than money!

And silence reigned;
The hall was warm with breathing;
And all the Soviet land
Stood behind that girl.[10]

The play in question was almost certainly the 1948 revival of Aleksandra Brushtein's *Uncle Tom*, evidently the most widely performed of her *Tom* iterations.[11] The revival coincided with an intensification of concern, not least among members of the US Communist left, with the problem of lynching and violence against black people, and this Brushtein rewriting found a way to reinflect the Tom story in light of that concern.[12] A self-reflexive frame narrative, set in the present, brackets the play: two black women, Dorothy and Cora, are walking to a movie theater when Cora is struck by a car driven by a white couple (Carson and Edith). Near the site of the hit-and-run crash is a large billboard depicting a lynched black man with the legend, "Negro! Run away from this city!" As she lies dying, waiting futilely for help to arrive, Cora sees the light of the theater's marquee, announcing that the current attraction is none other than a film of *Uncle Tom's Cabin*. "Which cabin?" she asks, prompting Dorothy to recount Stowe's story, enacted as a flashback onstage. During the performance, a song (again, in Negro spiritual style) tells of "the terrible smell of rope around a human neck," and cinema takes over the stage at the conclusion when Legree's face appears on a huge screen to threateningly announce, in a neat fusion of fierce denunciation of racism, anticapitalist animus, and late-Stalinist paranoia: "Look at me, remember my name! I control the world and will control it forever!"[13]

Brushtein continued tinkering with the play almost until her death in 1968. Many features remained constant or received refinement, especially the comical business (the Birds, for instance, were made a thoroughly funny couple, complete with a butler carrying a crow on his shoulder, in the 1967 version) in its dissonant clash with scenes of cruelty (Mrs. Shelby, now "Julia" and a clone of Marie St. Clare, refusing to part with her jewels to save Uncle Tom; a harsh scene of slave abasement during the "auction"). One notices, however, that Brushtein came to conclude the play in darker and ever less triumphant tones, ultimately giving her final 1967 rewriting a bleak terminus seemingly at odds with socialist realism's canonical optimism. After Eliza's daughter ("Titmouse") and Cassy escape from Legree, Tom (as in Stowe) stays behind but refuses to betray his friends and suffers the consequences. Together with Aunt Chloe—an altogether more prominent and ultimately serious figure in Brushtein's rewritings, as in many of the old Tolstoyan and early Soviet adaptations, than in Stowe's novel—an abolitionist engineer named Clayton (a character derived from Stowe's *Dred*) arrives at Legree's plantation with $1,500, earned in part by Chloe's labors at the confectioner's, to redeem Tom; Clayton hands over the money just as Tom is being beaten to death. With Clayton looking on helplessly and Legree standing unpunished onstage, Chloe sobs out the play's last words:

> CHLOE: Tom . . . Tom . . . [*sees Legree*] Murderer! Murderer! May the
> sun never shine upon you! May you never have water, nor fire, nor
> joy, nor a decent death! May you be damned, murderer! Damned!
> Damned!
> [*Curtain*][14]

The raging sorrow and anger of this ending is startling in the way that the crueler Eisenstein "attractions"—the Teutonic Knights hurling Russian babies onto a flaming pyre in *Alexander Nevsky* (1938), for instance—are startling, and doubtless unbalances both play and spectator. Brushtein's father, Iakov Vygodsky, briefly a member of the Vilnius *Judenrat* (Jewish Council) under the Nazis, had been arrested, tortured, and murdered by the SS in 1941, at the age of eighty-four: could that enormity, and the playwright's response to it, also be allegorized here?[15] The catastrophe of the Holocaust was not openly representable in the USSR, given official "national" narratives about the war and unofficial but widespread anti-Semitism, but knowing the fate of Brushtein's family, it is difficult not to think of it when reading this late reworking of *Tom*, possibly the last truly "anti-Fascist" version of the story produced in the Soviet Union. (Meanwhile, as it turns out, the US literary scene was witnessing [in David Bromwich's words] "a general rejection of agitational art and the program advanced a generation earlier by the Popular Front against Fascism" in favor of a more "autonomous" or modernist mode of humanist writing—a shift exemplified by James Baldwin's famous 1949 attack on both Stowe and Richard Wright.)[16] Again, as in the nineteenth century, as for Marina Tsvetaeva, questions loom about the salience and applicability of Stowe's novel: Does *Uncle Tom's Cabin* refer to the US past, the US present, the fascist past, the Soviet present? Does the novel's ideological exploitation again enable otherwise discouraged or forbidden kinds of memorialization?[17]

Silence was not an exclusive Soviet prerogative, to be sure, and *Tom* prefaces written on the US side of the Cold War divide from the forties through the sixties are less than frank about the continuing realities of segregation, discrimination, and racist violence. I have not conducted a thorough search, but of three prefaces I read, published between 1938 and 1961—by Raymond Weaver, Langston Hughes, and Van Wyck Brooks—not one of them utters a peep about any ongoing "problems" on the racial front in America. Brooks actually concludes his essay on the following jolly note:

> Almost a century after the question of slavery had been settled, *Uncle Tom's Cabin* remained a readable and even exciting book, a true panorama of American Society, fair to the South as well as to the North, generous and humane in its feeling and its portraiture. It even foresaw the Africa of our day with republics growing there "with the rapidity of tropical vegetation."[18]

That Hughes also failed to break the silence suggests that there were indeed considerable pressures (some unconscious, others perhaps more direct) to not speak of this topic. In 1938 he had written a parody for the stage of Stowe's novel titled *Colonel Tom's Cabin*, in which a left-leaning Tom abandons all servility and ends up administering a slap to Little Eva.[19] It is hard to believe that the concluding sentence of his later preface—where he states that "the love and warmth and humanity that went into [the] writing [of *Uncle Tom's Cabin*] keep it alive a century later from Bombay to Boston"—adequately represents his actual judgment of the novel.[20]

Already by 1950, and more noticeably after Stalin's death, the rhetoric of the Soviet prefaces are softened somewhat and tend to follow a fairly predictable pattern. A brief account of Stowe's life, of US slavery, and of the Civil War period is given, followed by an appreciation of the novel that stresses its polemical effect in the 1850s, its exposure of the horrors of slavery, and its power to rouse feelings not only of sympathy but also of "deep hatred" toward those "whose fault it is that good, hard-working people like Uncle Tom perish still today—toward the American capitalists."[21] Of course, at some point the prefaces always reproach Stowe for "the partial nature of her solutions, her tendency to compromise," and her discovery of "a way out of the existing situation through Christian religion rather than armed struggle."[22] Reference is often made to American criticisms of "Uncle Tomism," sometimes to the book's reliance on cliché, although virtually never to its blatant racial hierarchy. Finally, there is a turn to the contemporary US situation, comprised of accounts (in varying detail) of contemporary American racism (segregation, Klan violence, exclusion of African Americans from educational and other institutions) and of the new status of the moniker "Uncle Tom" as a curse for African Americans. Some of the earlier postwar editions also include an implied call to "working people of the world" to fight for happiness "through their own struggle and their own labor," but these hortatory gestures vanish over time, to be replaced by a more generalized humanistic tone.[23] We find many variants rung on these basic changes, but these are the essential topoi of the Cold War *Tom* preface.

Most intriguing is the fact that the majority of the translations to which these prefaces are appended are children's versions from which most of the religion has already been purged. There is a subtle paradox at work here, because while the story of Uncle Tom is selected as edifying material for kids precisely because of its power to "excite strong emotions and exalted feelings," a preface is required in order to qualify the sentimental attachment that might develop in relation to Stowe's pacifist hero, as well as to undo the sense that Uncle Tom is in any way typical of contemporary African Americans.[24] (None of the postwar editions go so far as to make George Harris the hero, however.) Again, an attempt is made to retain the moral-emotional power of Stowe's tale while harnessing and contextualizing it in new, un-Stowe-like ways. This is not to say, of course, that the book was not frequently read independently of the prefaces and therefore of official frameworks for its interpretation.

The great "Soviet humanist" version of *Uncle Tom's Cabin* is undoubtedly the abridged translation by Natalia A. Volzhina, which first appeared in 1950.[25] This translation quickly became essentially the only Russian *Uncle Tom* available, a situation that has turned it into the de facto standard version for Russian readers; in the year 2000, this same 1950 edition (with very minor stylistic alterations and without a preface) was published by the St. Petersburg children's publisher "ABC" (Azbuka).[26] From what I can tell, nearly every edition of *Uncle Tom's Cabin* published in Russian since 1950 (at least fifteen in number, doubtless many more) bears Volzhina's name, although those editions differ in terms of completeness, as we shall see. Eventually released in millions of copies, the Volzhina version is certainly one of the most widely read renderings of Stowe's novel ever.

Volzhina's translation has a fluency and idiomatic directness (with no "Russian peasant" embroidery) that no doubt helped to secure it a broad audience. It also manages to Sovietize and sanitize Stowe without placing any obvious strain on the text or resorting to didactic supplements. Most of the changes are simply cuts and are often indicated with ellipsis marks (three asterisks on a separate line): the whole scene of worship during the "Evening in Uncle Tom's Cabin" and the religious assurances provided after Legree "[smites] his victim to the ground" (Stowe, 421) are removed in this fashion.[27] Some unseemly passages are excised more covertly, as (for example) when Stowe has St. Clare impolitely compare the influence of "vicious, improvident, degraded" slaves on slaveholders' children to smallpox (Stowe, 240).[28] Virtually all of Stowe's Christian interjections are elided (though not all pious exclamations by characters in the novel), as is Tom's vision of "one crowned with thorns, buffeted and bleeding" (Stowe, 399). Instead, the inner lives of the characters become motions of sentiment alone:

> "Well, aren't you a fool!" Legree spat in Tom's face, kicked him, but before leaving said: "All right! You'll be on your knees before me yet, just you watch!"
>
> Tom sat for a long time by the fire, struggling with himself internally. Suddenly his eyes were fogged over; he stretched his arm out into the darkness and fell down unconscious.
>
> Tom did not know how long this oblivion lasted. When he came to, the fire was already out, and his clothes were soaked through with dew—but all his doubts had vanished, and such joy came upon his soul that nothing was frightening to him—neither hunger, nor cold, nor humiliation, nor loneliness.[29]

It is unclear, of course, whether the shape of the 1950 version is due to Volzhina or the editor, M. Lorie. At some point, Volzhina did translate the book in its entirety, and this translation (with only the topical though still important "Concluding Remarks" omitted) appeared in a very large edition (five hundred thousand copies!) in 1977, with no preface or "guides to interpretation" of any kind.[30] As usual, the extratextual reasons for this anomaly (which was not, however, the last Soviet edition of this version) are difficult to pin down, but 1977 was arguably the high point of the so-called détente between the superpowers, right before the turn to a more hostile US policy (inaugurated under Zbigniew Brzezinski during the Carter administration) and prior to the USSR's increasingly provocative support of revolutionaries in Angola, Ethiopia, and Nicaragua and its fateful invasion of Afghanistan on Christmas Eve, 1979.[31] It might have been thought that *Uncle Tom's Cabin* had become by this time a fairly harmless "classic of American literature" and worthy of fuller, less polemical presentation.

To be sure, Stowe's novel had been largely normalized as a canonical presence for the Soviet reading public, certainly through integration into school and university curricula but via other forms of mass-cultural dissemination as well, such as Brushtein's adaptations and, in at least one intriguing instance, on film.[32] An epic production of *Uncle Tom's Cabin* directed by the Hungarian filmmaker Géza von Radványi (1907–86)—best known for his 1947 drama *Somewhere in Europe*, a powerful neorealist work (scripted by famous film theorist Béla Balázs) about children orphaned by war—appeared at the Fourth Moscow International Film Festival in 1965 and was released to Soviet audiences the following summer. This French-German-Italian-Yugoslav coproduction was the first large-scale cinematic *Tom* made anywhere in almost forty years, shot in 70 mm with six-track stereo and an international if somewhat oddly tossed-together cast, including singers Eartha Kitt and Juliette Greco, a number of Europe-based US expat actors such as John Kitzmiller (Tom), Olive Moorehead (Cassy), and Charles Fawcett (Mr. Shelby), and starring Herbert Lom, later famous as the maniacally squinting Commissioner Dreyfus in the Pink Panther films and at the time a mainstay of popular UK cinema, in the role of a suave-yet-nasty Simon Legree.[33]

More Mephisto than brute, Lom's Legree is present in the film almost from beginning to end and fuses together many of the unattractive slave owners and slave traders in the book, while adding numerous malevolent touches of his own. His sensationally evil deeds include

Figure 6. Herbert Lom (Simon Legree) and John Kitzmiller (Tom), in a publicity still for Géza von Radványi's film *Onkel Toms Hütte* [*Uncle Tom's Cabin*], 1965.

shooting St. Clare and blaming the crime on a black waiter (who is duly lynched by a white mob) and allowing a slave attempting escape to be eaten by a crocodile, an event witnessed by a whole Mississippi-steamboat-load of people (including Little Eva and Uncle Tom, who remain dry the entire time).

Sex is played up even more than in Stowe, with the Cassy-Legree relation taking up much screen time, and Little Eva dying largely due to her shock at seeing her father passionately and adulterously kissing a beautiful houseguest of the St. Clares (a character not in the novel, played by bombshell du jour Mylène Demongeot). There was, of course, a long tradition of massaging the novel in order to extract from it maximum entertainment value, although this was not, in the main, the

Soviet tradition. Joining the international film festival circuit means bringing in foreign films, however, and one small effect of the USSR's thaw-era entry into that circuit (in 1959 with the first Moscow festival) was the exposure of Soviet audiences to a more lurid, sexed-up, spaghetti-westernized version of *Tom*, a belated and oblique gust from the "Tom show" heritage of which Russians had but little knowledge.[34]

The film plays inconsistently with anachronism as well, in part to suggest Stowe's contemporary relevance: most obviously on the level of the funk-jazz inflected and often unintentionally hilarious score, but also in a prologue that moves backward from overhead shots of the Statue of Liberty and Manhattan to the Lincoln Memorial and on to corny restagings of Lincoln's legendary meeting with Stowe and his assassination (a tilt of the camera reveals that the president had been reading *Uncle Tom's Cabin*, in German, in Ford's Theater). Indeed, a subtextual "assassination" theme runs through the film and is brought to the surface when Legree shoots St. Clare, who is getting out of his carriage in the midst of Independence Day festivities, from an upper-story window of a hotel—a mise-en-scène surely meant to remind audiences in the mid-1960s of the 1963 assassination of John F. Kennedy.[35] Unfortunately, I do not know what Soviet audiences thought of Radványi's *Tom*; although it presents itself as a serious and "contemporary" work, the film's titillating stress on sex and violence was certainly at odds with Soviet conventions for presenting Stowe's narrative. Those emphases may also have (uncomfortably?) brought to the surface aspects of the *Tom* story that had always been part of its appeal.[36]

Radványi's extraction of serious, "adult" themes from *Uncle Tom's Cabin* was additionally unusual insofar as the text had long been comfortably assigned to the category of "children's literature," in the Soviet context as elsewhere. The majority of editions appearing during what turned out to be the twilight years of the 1970s and 1980s were repeats of the earlier, shorter Volzhina version, again packaged for children. Then in 1990, well after the peak years of glasnost euphoria and on the cusp of the Soviet Union's final collapse, *Uncle Tom's Cabin* appeared in the Volzhina translation with the final chapter included. This was therefore the first—and, as it turned out, the last—complete version of the novel to appear in Russian during the lifetime of the USSR.[37] The introduction to this edition (by A. Nikoliukin) is far more circumspect than earlier prefaces and criticizes earlier rejections of the nonviolent "Uncle Tom way" in a manner that recalls Raisa Orlova's defense of Tom's stance of refusal. Referring to both Thoreau's and

Tolstoy's notions of civil disobedience and adding a new religious inflection, Nikoliukin compares Tom with those who insist that revolt is possible only "with a weapon in one's hands":

> In a battle the winner is always the one who conquers. In [the other case], carried out with mildness and patience, the only blood that flows is one's own; Uncle Tom dies, but the victory, the real spiritual victory remains his. [There] is no question of whether the one who conquers is not ultimately a worse evil than the one who is conquered—and this is a problem that all those who have risen in revolt must sooner or later resolve.[38]

A profound melancholy about the fate of the revolutionary project is unmistakable here, and suggests a basis for some new, as-yet-unformulated post-Soviet reading of Tom as (again) a neo-Tolstoyan hero.

Coda: Tom, Meet Scarlett

A<small>LTHOUGH STANDARD</small> (i.e., condensed) Volzhina versions are occasionally republished, and at least one entirely new translation has appeared since 2000, religious publishing houses have begun releasing their own editions of *Uncle Tom's Cabin*, sometimes selecting from among the many prerevolutionary options, properly aware of the distortions in the Soviet editions.[1] I tend to doubt, however, whether the new (and far from universal) interest in religion assures the book much of a future among Russian readers. The post-Soviet order has introduced (among many other things) a whole host of new cultural commodities to the public, including new representations of the United States and of African Americans; these last can only work to relativize Stowe's particular vision, which is not a bad thing.

Moreover, it may be that Russian imaginings of the period and place described by Stowe are now being shaped by another novel that has gained colossal popularity and acclaim since around 1989. Margaret Mitchell's 1936 *Gone with the Wind*, the best-selling historical novel of all time, first appeared in Russian translation in the USSR in 1982, although Soviet cultural authorities and probably many readers knew of it long before.[2] No doubt some combination of contempt for the novel's pop-fictional reputation and rejection of its flagrant racism and reactionary politics had prevented a prior Soviet appearance (although it is not entirely clear why it was first published in the pre-glasnost year of 1982).[3] The real Mitchell boom began at decade's end: between 1989 and 1993, at least sixty-nine different editions of *Wind*, published everywhere in large print runs from Kiev to Vologda and from Briansk to Tashkent, blew across the soon-to-be-former and former Soviet Union. (Meanwhile, somewhere around ten editions of *Uncle Tom's Cabin* have been published in Russia since 1989.) Although the proliferation of editions fell off drastically after 1993, "[*Gone with the Wind*] and the sequel to it written by Alexandra Ripley [*Scarlett*, 1991]," as historian Stephen Lovell writes, "proved the greatest success story of post-Soviet publishing."[4]

We might well expect that the Old South and anti-Reconstruction mythologies purveyed by Mitchell's novel would have an effect on Russian perceptions of the United States and the US past (and perhaps the Russian past as well)—unfortunately. My own sense, however, is that the reasons for its popularity are better sought in the twin, changing contexts of readership/publishing, on the one hand, and large-scale societal breakdown, on the other. *Gone with the Wind* is a hybrid work that potentially functions in a variety of genres and on a number of brow levels simultaneously. It can thus be seen as another "vanishing mediator," rather like Mitchell's nemesis *Uncle Tom* in this respect, that attracted audiences who liked adventure stories, who were coming to like the relatively new romance genre—"in 1991, Barbara Cartland overtook Stalin as the most published author ever [in the Soviet Union]"—and those who liked, or thought they should like, the serious and prestigious form of the historical novel.[5] (Although many Russian editions of *Gone with the Wind* are wrapped in familiar "romance novel" covers—lurid color, bare-chested hunk embracing almost equally bare-chested woman, and so on—the book has also been issued as a classy mock-leather-bound volume in the series The Golden Archive of World Classics, alongside works by Cervantes, Goethe, and Balzac.)[6] Indeed, not only later historians but also prefacers at the time were aware of the potential cross-genre appeal of the book.[7] Meanwhile, established Soviet publishing houses, accustomed to monopoly and nonmarket distribution, were having a difficult time surviving in the early nineties; Mitchell's was among the works that helped keep some of them afloat (*Pravda* released a big edition in 1986).

On the level of the novel's "content," my own sense—partially derived from conversations with Russians who have read the book, and therefore anecdotal, if concrete—is that Russian readers encountering *Gone with the Wind* in the late eighties and early nineties were captivated above all by the figure of Scarlett O'Hara in her struggles both against conformist pressures and to preserve her family home, Tara. As Louis Rubin Jr. has noted, the underlying ideology of *Gone with the Wind* is notably materialist rather than metaphysical or idealist, in its valorization of Scarlett's marital and business entrepreneurship:

> The statement has often been made, by [Margaret Mitchell] herself among others, that Scarlett O'Hara does what she does in order to survive, with the implication that had it not been for the need to sweat and scheme in order to survive, she would have been better off, happier, more contented. . . . [Yet] the reverse is more like the truth: she was deeply dissatisfied under the old regime, and the effect of the war and the destruction of the plantation system was to liberate her from the constriction of her traditional role as Southern lady. . . . What Scarlett O'Hara does in postwar Atlanta . . . is . . . no more and no less than what the South as a whole did in the late nineteenth century and is still doing in the twentieth century. It is what a middle-class, democratic, capitalistic society always does: try to make money and improve its position.[8]

Rubin understates the importance of the survival theme in the novel, but his analysis hits on what was surely a fundamental feature of *Wind*'s appeal in the Russia of the early nineties: the idea that hard-nosed practical action, and specifically women's hard-nosed practical action, can pull individuals and families out of catastrophe, whether that be the Soviet past, the collapse of the Soviet Union, the attendant social chaos, or (more probably) all three. (And again, Russian commentators at the time noted the centrality to the book of both civilizational crisis and the emergence of a new set of material [capitalist] relations out of crisis.)[9] At a moment of demographic collapse, precipitous decline in standard of living, evaporation of social services, contraction of educational infrastructure, soaring crime and corruption rates, and a sudden shift to "market relations," Mitchell's novel met an ideal audience— rather like it had on its first appearance, in the midst of the Great Depression.[10]

Conclusion

SCARLETT AND UNCLE TOM, matter and spirit: no two protagonists could be less compatible. Might the shift from Stowe to Mitchell be symptomatic of a fundamental mutation within Russian attitudes toward literate culture as such? As Stephen Lovell notes,

> For the first time in 130 years . . . the reader was no longer a subject of impassioned debate, a rhetorical weapon, a myth, or a mystery; rather, he or she became "simply" a socio-economic reality.[1]

Our examination of *Uncle Tom* in Russia has not only demonstrated that Russian reading culture has always been complexly configured, with multiple imperatives—commercial, artistic, educational, ideological, geopolitical, self-representational—struggling for space; it has also shown that Stowe's novel has a distinctive, perhaps unique power to draw those imperatives to the surface. Yet that power may now be exhausted, save perhaps the attractions that *Uncle Tom* will still exert on historians, literary scholars, and other writers of academic books (like this one).

It would seem that today's educated elites neither wish to claim a work like *Uncle Tom's Cabin* as their own—stained as it is by Soviet appropriations, not to mention Stowe's own expressions of anticapitalism—nor possess the resources or will to continue on with "enlightenment," whether religiously or atheistically inflected. Indeed, the historian Edward Acton has cogently argued that even the traditional conceptual vocabulary of intellectual activism has been lost:

> [The Communist Party] had projected Soviet socialism as the culmination of human progress, the fulfillment of man's aspiration for social

justice, altruism, democracy, liberty, equality, international fraternity, solidarity and peace. Each claim, it is true, rang ever more hollow. But the effect was not only to create deep cynicism about the regime but to jaundice an entire discourse, to debase the language of social analysis and historical progress. Nor, after two world wars and the horrors of the Holocaust, did the West provide any equivalent of the overarching explanatory models, optimistic philosophies of history and novel conceptual tools on which the pre-revolutionary intelligentsia had drawn. There, too, the Enlightenment project was in crisis, and neither the resurgence of fundamentalist faith in free-market individualism nor the intellectual pirouette of post-modernism had much resonance in the Soviet context.[2]

No one would question the importance of pragmatic struggles to make a living in a changed economic environment or to make electoral practices under the Putinist state more democratic; yet these do not (yet) seem projects that require the electric vision of *absolute* justice and injustice that informs Stowe's novel and guides the actions of her main protagonist. Prior to saying "goodbye to Uncle Tom," though, we might try to get a better (or at least a more *open*) sense of the novel's prospects, while hopefully avoiding vain prophecies, via a brief summation of its reception in Russia so far—or rather, of that reception's salient conditions of possibility.

First, we have seen that the reception of *Uncle Tom's Cabin* in Russia—as elsewhere, but with very specific inflections molded by the country's imperial, dynastic, and rural-patriarchal character and the cosmopolitanism of its elites—has been conditioned by three large-scale historical forces that together began to take on recognizable shape by the late eighteenth–beginning of the nineteenth centuries: the development of commerce, in particular the emergence of the book and journal trade and the slow growth of an entrepreneurial class; the gradual rise of the nation-state as a universal form of social belonging; and a new drive, doubtless influenced by earlier political movements like Quaker abolitionism, toward a radical universalization of equality and liberty, beyond the limited if wide-ranging prescriptions offered by revolutionary documents like the *Declaration of the Rights of Man and the Citizen* (1789).[3] To be sure, all these forces interact complexly over time and in diverse ways—ranging from state censorship of the press to "dissident" struggles for rights (whether in the nineteenth or the twentieth century) to imaginings of "national" literature, visual art, and music, invariably within a comparative, cosmopolitan framework—even as distinguishing them helps to give conceptual shape to the reception of Stowe's novel.

For if we think about that reception, it is helpful in turn to extract from it three primary *functions* that *Uncle Tom's Cabin* was purported to have (or not have). Stowe's novel was supposed to be, above all, *a prompt and guide to right (ethical, political) conduct*, whether through its critical analysis of slavery (Nikolai Turgenev, Chernyshevsky), its representation of exemplary characters and their antitypes (the censor A. Smirnov, Gorbunov-Posadov), or through its power to awaken feelings of sympathy for other human beings (Khomyakov, Tolstoy). Not less importantly, the book was also *an occasion for learning*: most fundamentally, learning to read (a value much extolled in Stowe's own pages), but also learning about slavery (and sometimes serfdom) as a system, and about the lives of other peoples far distant, above all those of the United States (Gorbunov-Posadov, and most if not all of the Soviet prefacers and adapters). Finally, *Uncle Tom's Cabin* was *a work of literature*, a much-read if controversial one, and as such a model or counter-model for writers hoping to participate in the creation of a national (which also implies *internationally recognized*) literature (Turgenev, Tolstoy, Fet, and the editors of the Soviet *Literary Encyclopedia*, all in different ways). Receptions differed depending on how these ethical, educational, and literary functions were subsumed under the rubrics of nation-state developmental imperatives, commercial goals, or emancipatory political aspirations; these rubrics invariably overlapped and often conflicted.

This is simply to say that the functions of Stowe's novel need to be considered dialectically, in terms of reception as a field of struggle and debate, rather than as static textual features. Think, for instance, of Pisarev's claim that the failings of *Uncle Tom's Cabin* as literature (but also as fact-based reportage) undo its ethical-political project; or the later Tolstoy's opposite insistence that the book's affective and moral power *is* its literary value; or N. V. Chekhov extolling *Uncle Tom* as useful reading for children, while denying it any serious literary status; or the evident nervousness of some of the early Soviet translators/adapters about how "functional" the book remained at all; and so on.

Clearly enough, these receptions are in turn shaped by the way that the various historical forces exerting themselves on writers and readers find ideological expression. Thus the censor Smirnov, a mid-nineteenth-century cultural manager, conceives of Stowe's novel as appropriate reading (especially in its provision of suitable role models and harsh depiction of US slavery) for *Russian* peasants moving a step closer toward something like participation in a national public; thus the Tolstoyans of Posrednik see *Uncle Tom's Cabin* as a way of squaring the circle between market, moral-ethical, and educational values, while retaining some autonomy from the state and from the commercial book trade alike; thus an editor from the prerevolutionary educated elite, seeking to enlighten both people and state within the framework of the state-approved press, could rework the depiction of Augustine St. Clare into a suitable exemplar for that elite; thus the early Soviet adapters could replace Stowe's universal ethic of justice (Christianity) with their own (Communism), while (like their prerevolutionary predecessors) not entirely managing to avoid overlap with another universalizing framework of value structuring Stowe's novel (racism).[4]

In some ways, the Soviet case is an extreme and special one, where we find a never-fully-realized attempt by the party-state to collapse the entire field of collective value and agency—production, circulation, and distribution (here, of texts); state-national hegemony and institutions; and universalist and emancipatory political aspirations—into a single configuration, with the Communist Party at the center. Hence, the paradoxes of a political discourse entirely statist, patriotic (even ethno-centrically patriotic), and radically "equalitarian" (on an international level) at the same time; hence the Soviet use of *Uncle Tom's Cabin* at once to critique racial inequality, to attack its Cold War geopolitical nemesis on the field of "grand strategy," and to participate in the global literary sphere, even while concealing or distorting (through its monopoly of publishing) whole dimensions of Stowe's book at odds with its own supposedly universalist ideology and socialist practice. (In another way, of course, these paradoxes are merely the burdens of being one of two "superpowers.") The ironies of this configuration are perhaps best exemplified by the situation of Efim Etkind in 1949: a Soviet Jewish intellectual writing an overheated afterword to *Uncle Tom's Cabin* during the late Stalin-era anti-Semitic campaign, thereby managing to critique American racism, demonstrate Soviet patriotism (rather than "cosmopolitanism"), and engage as a professional scholar with a certain discourse of "world literature" all at once.[5]

Today struggles for human rights continue to be deeply mediated and/or confounded by the entwined universalities of the market and the nation-state framework, in Russia as everywhere else. In such a context,

Uncle Tom's Cabin might well remain a dusty old classic and minor cultural commodity; could it become topical, energize a mass reception, again? I have my doubts, but allow me a concluding proposal.

Stowe's novel grew on the soil of conflicts over labor, and *that* ground certainly remains a fertile source of social contradiction, even in our own age of (in Étienne Balibar's phrase) "real universality."[6] I am thinking now about the problems facing workers in the Russian context: citizens of the Russian Federation, to be sure, set adrift on the world market to sell their labor power; but also the country's enormous population of migrant laborers, mainly from former Soviet republics—a *Gastarbeiter* population second only to that of the United States in size, profoundly important to the national economy, a target of discrimination both de jure and de facto, and very much unleashed as a "social force" by the collapse of the old Communist system and the emergence of new market relations.[7]

On a political-ethical level, *Uncle Tom's Cabin* is a book about the injustice of slavery, an ongoing injustice that destroys the bonds of family, friendship, and life itself. But on another level both formal and historical, and despite its reputation as a work centering on the domestic, it is in many ways a book about *borders* and the crossing of borders, beginning with the cross-border crisis that occasioned its composition in the first place: the Fugitive Slave Law, that most compromised statute of the Compromise of 1850, which made it illegal for northerners to harbor escaped slaves. The flight of Eliza and little Harry across the half-frozen Ohio River, the most often illustrated (and parodied) scene in the novel, is the iconic instance, but we can also think of Eliza and George's escape to Canada, to France, and eventually to the "refuge in Africa," the nation-state of Liberia (Stowe, 453); the utopian space of the Quaker settlement, site of hospitality and resistance; the very different journeys of the northerners Miss Ophelia and Simon Legree to the South; the horrifying stories of Emmeline, Cassy, Prue, and many others, as they and their families are moved from one place to another as enslaved commodities; and Tom, "the Man That Was a Thing," who is ultimately granted some vision of "other worlds" (Stowe, 427), but whose trip to Legree's plantation Stowe explicitly compares with the primordial migration: "The Middle Passage" (title of vol. 2, chap. 31).[8] In changed form, the dialectics of migration and labor that *Uncle Tom's Cabin* was one of the first books to explore are still as central to the lives of Russians, and everyone else, as they were to those of Stowe and her contemporaries, even as the ideological boundary lines of race that so confound Stowe's egalitarian vision continue to transect all these territorial crossings, returns, wanderings, and confinements.[9]

Do we see here the germs of a new reading of *Uncle Tom's Cabin*, appropriate (if not adequate) to the age of neoliberalism? Perhaps, but such a reading would certainly take us beyond the bounds of either Russia or the United States and into the wider world where, as we have seen, *Uncle Tom's Cabin* has always really belonged.

Appendix: Summary of Uncle Tom's Cabin

Seriously in debt and at risk of losing his property, a farmer from Kentucky named Arthur Shelby unwillingly contracts to sell two of his slaves—Uncle Tom, his pious, kindly farm manager; and a lively, attractive young boy named Harry, son of Mrs. Shelby's quadroon maid Eliza and her husband, the light-skinned slave and inventor George Harris—to a slave trader named Haley. Eliza overhears discussion of the planned sale and, after informing Uncle Tom and his wife, Aunt Chloe, heads to the North with Harry, hoping to rejoin George, who had just fled for Canada. Although he supports Eliza's decision to escape and has a wife and several children of his own, Uncle Tom resolves to obey his master and submits to being sold. Shelby's son, who is also named George and is deeply attached to Uncle Tom, vows to buy Tom back; Aunt Chloe takes up work at a confectioner's in order to help raise the payment.

Haley pursues Eliza, but she escapes in a hair-raising crossing of the half-frozen Ohio River, which separated southern slave territory from the North. She and Harry eventually make it to a Quaker settlement, after being harbored by a US senator named Bird and his wife— ironically, the senator had just voted in favor of the passage of the Fugitive Slave Law (1850), which made harboring escaped slaves illegal in the North—and are joined there by Eliza's husband, George Harris.

Meanwhile, Haley has both hired a group of slave hunters headed by the brutish Tom Loker to capture Eliza and Harry and dispatched Uncle Tom on a Mississippi riverboat to be sold at a slave auction downstream. On the boat, Tom befriends a cherubic and charismatic little white girl named Eva, who is traveling back to New Orleans with her father, a wealthy, good-hearted, witty, and somewhat jaded and

103

melancholic estate owner named Augustine St. Clare. After Tom saves Eva from drowning, St. Clare buys him and takes him to his New Orleans mansion.

Uncle Tom lives on the estate for two years, becoming indispensable to the running of the estate and close to both St. Clare and, especially, the devout Eva, with whom he reads the Bible. Miss Ophelia, St. Clare's cousin from Vermont, visits during this time and tries to bring some New England orderliness and thrift to the "shiftless" St. Clare household.

Back in the North, Loker and his men attempt to capture Eliza and Harry but are faced down in an armed confrontation. George Harris shoots Loker in the side, and the escaped slaves flee to another Quaker settlement, bringing along the wounded Loker.

On the St. Clare estate, St. Clare and Ophelia discuss slavery and race. Opposed to slavery, Ophelia reveals in her discussions with St. Clare—who hates slavery, and argues powerfully against it in debate with his brother, Alfred, but despairs of ever being able to do anything about it—that she also harbors negative attitudes toward black people. St. Clare, who carries no such hostility, tries to cure Ophelia of her prejudices by buying her a slave girl, the rowdy and energetic Topsy, to educate.

Eva becomes ill and dies, and her death has a great impact on the household: Miss Ophelia loses her hostility toward black people; Topsy becomes trusting, honest and mature; and the heartbroken St. Clare resolves to set Uncle Tom free. Before he has a chance to free Tom, however, he is stabbed to death while trying to mediate a brawl in a tavern. Although St. Clare accepts Christ on his deathbed, his heartless and egotistical wife, Marie, sells all the slaves after his death, and Tom ends up the property of Simon Legree, a vicious and sadistic plantation owner originally from the North.

While on Legree's plantation, Tom comes to know Emmeline, a young slave woman bought by Legree to be his mistress, and Cassy, a slave woman who has been Legree's mistress for some time. Cassy's suffering and disappointments, particularly the loss of her children, have embittered her, and Tom's own faith is sorely tried both by his conversations with Cassy and his physical and spiritual ordeal on Legree's plantation. Tom's piety, kindness, and refusal to beat other slaves antagonize Legree, who had envisioned using Tom as an overseer, and Tom becomes the target of his wrath. Tom is given two visions, however—one of Eva and one of Christ—which sustain him after being severely beaten by Legree and the overseers.

Around this time, George, Eliza, and Harry finally escape to Canada with the help of Loker, who has repented of his slave-hunting past.

Cassy and Emmeline come up with a ruse (involving getting dressed up as ghosts) to escape from Legree. After their escape, Legree interrogates Tom: when Tom refuses to give information on the whereabouts of the fugitives, Legree and two overseers beat him brutally. George Shelby, who has meanwhile gathered enough money to buy Tom, arrives just in time to see the martyred Tom die.

Cassy and Emmeline travel north on a boat and meet George Harris's sister, who goes with them to Canada. Upon meeting George and Eliza, Cassy realizes that Eliza is actually her daughter, sold away long ago. Now united as a family, the former slaves travel to France and thence to Liberia, the African colony-nation created for former US slaves; George Harris resolves to help build a Christian society there. George Shelby returns to Kentucky and, in honor of Uncle Tom, frees all the Shelby slaves after his father's death, exhorting them to be "as honest and faithful and Christian as [Tom] was."

Notes

Introduction

1. I sometimes use the term "Russo-Soviet" rather than "Soviet" in this study to indicate its restriction (due to the limits of my own linguistic competence, in part) to Russian-language versions of/responses to Stowe's novel during the lifetime of the Soviet Union (1922-91). The novel was widely read in Russian in Soviet republics outside the USSR's Russian "cosmopolitan center," however, and editions in other Soviet languages no doubt shared features characteristic of the Russo-Soviet versions (discussed later).

All translations are my own unless otherwise noted. In the main text and index, I use familiar English renderings of Russian names (e.g., Chernyshevsky); for purposes of bibliographical accuracy and to make it easier to trace sources, I use a more formal transcription system in the endnotes (e.g., Chernyshevskij).

2. The same comment (minus the reference to Feuchtwanger's novel) appears in a letter written the same day by Tsvetaeva to Ariadna Berg (*Sobranie sochinenij*, 7:532).

3. See Razumovsky, *Marina Tsvetaeva*, 278-300. Sergei and Ariadna Efron had become Soviet sympathizers while in France; Sergei fled to the USSR after falling under suspicion of being involved in the murder of Soviet defector Ignatij Rejss (1899-1937). Ariadna Efron (1912-75) had a miscarriage after being beaten by the secret police; she had been the first to return to the USSR, in March 1937, and was incarcerated twice by the regime (1939-47; 1949-55).

4. See Mamatey and Luzha, *History of the Czechoslovak Republic*, 239-52.

5. Tsvetaeva wrote nine more letters to Tesková (out of at least 120); the last was written on 12 June 1939, just before Tsvetaeva's departure for the USSR. Previous letters refer explicitly to the Czech-German situation. See *Sobranie sochinenij*, 6:467-80.

6. See Pehle, *November 1938*.

7. On Tsvetaeva's fusings/blurrings of conventional gender distinctions in her writing, see the chapter "The Death of the Poetess" in Boym, *Death in Quotation Marks*, esp. 210. Although Tsvetaeva is not usually thought of as an "activist" writer, her poems to Czechoslovakia (written around the same time) are in fact full of calls for armed resistance.

8. "Poem of the End," in Tsvetaeva, *Selected Poems*, 86–87. Though translated by Feinstein as "Jews," the last word of the section (*zhidy*, rather than *evrei* [Jews]) is, in Russian, quite unambiguous in meaning.

9. For producing and disseminating what was termed "anti-Soviet propaganda," Sinyavsky and Daniel were tried and sentenced in February 1966 to incarceration in labor camps for seven and five years, respectively; their trial and conviction helped provoke the rise of dissidence in the USSR. See Suny, *Soviet Experiment*, 421–34.

10. While writing the comment quoted in the epigraph, Paustovsky might have had a famous remark on Stowe by one of his idols, Anton Chekhov, at the back of his mind. At the age of nineteen, Chekhov wrote in a letter to his brother Mikhail: "Did Madame Beecher Stowe bring tears to your eyes? I used to read her some time ago, but then about six months ago I read through her book in a spirit of research. After that I experienced the disagreeable sensation, familiar to mortals, of having overindulged in raisins and currants" (Chekhov, *Life in Letters*, 13–14).

11. For readers whose memory of the plot of *Uncle Tom's Cabin* could use some refreshing, please see my brief summary (appendix).

12. The phrase "epithet of servility" is Linda Williams's from her *Playing the Race Card*, 63. Among the more important mid-twentieth-century works to examine and critique the long arc of *Uncle Tom's Cabin*'s reception are F. Wilson, *Crusader in Crinoline*; Birdoff, *World's Greatest Hit*; James Baldwin's seminal essay "Everybody's Protest Novel," which fashioned a corrosive comparison of the polemical manipulativeness of Stowe's novel with that of Richard Wright's *Native Son* (1940), republished in *Notes of a Native Son*, 13–23; Furnas, *Goodbye to Uncle Tom*; E. Wilson, *Patriotic Gore*, esp. 3–58; and later, Thomas F. Gossett's grand summation, *Uncle Tom's Cabin and American Culture*. For three studies published during the same period that examine Russian serfdom and US slavery from a cultural and historical perspective, see Dow, "Seichas"; Hecht, "Russian Intelligentsia and American Slavery"; and Goldman, "American Slavery and Russian Serfdom."

13. The most celebrated and influential intervention was that of Tompkins: "Sentimental Power," reprinted in her *Sensational Designs*, 122–46. See also, among other works, Fisher, *Hard Facts*, esp. 87–127; Sundquist, *New Essays on Uncle Tom's Cabin*; Brown, *Domestic Individualism*, esp. 13–60; Brodhead, *Cultures of Letters*, esp. 13–47; Lott, *Love and Theft*, esp. 211–33; Hedrick, *Harriet Beecher Stowe*; Hartman, *Scenes of Subjection*; M. Wood, *Blind Memory*; Noble, *Masochistic Pleasures of Sentimental Literature*; L. Williams, *Playing the Race Card*; Meer, *Uncle*

Tom Mania; Weinstein, *Cambridge Companion to Harriet Beecher Stowe*; Ammons, *Harriet Beecher Stowe's Uncle Tom's Cabin*; Greven, *Men beyond Desire*, esp. 153–92; Parfait, *Publishing History of Uncle Tom's Cabin*; Morgan, *Uncle Tom's Cabin as Visual Culture*; the essays included in Stowe, *Uncle Tom's Cabin: Authoritative Text, Backgrounds and Contexts, Criticism*; Reynolds, *Mightier than the Sword*; and Hochman, *Uncle Tom's Cabin and the Reading Revolution*.

14. On the British response, see F. Wilson, *Crusader in Crinoline*, 302, 325–30, 362–93; Gossett, *Uncle Tom's Cabin and American Culture*, 239–59; and Meer, *Uncle Tom Mania*. On the French and German, see Lucas, *La littérature anti-esclavagiste au dix-neuvième siècle*; and Maclean, *Uncle Tom's Cabin in Germany*. For a fascinating recent essay on the reception of Stowe's novel in Italy, and specifically its impact as a ballet, see Körner, "Uncle Tom on the Ballet Stage." Michael Gibbs Hill discusses the role played by translations of Stowe's novel in late nineteenth and early twentieth century China in *Lin Shu, Inc.* The most important consideration of Stowe's work in an international context is Kohn, Meer, and Todd, *Transatlantic Stowe*. Intriguingly, at least three significant foreign-language studies of Stowe's novel appeared immediately prior to the *Tom* renaissance of the late 1970s: poet and essayist Roberto Friol's *En la cabaña del Tío Tom*, originally a sketch for a larger study of the influence of *Uncle Tom's Cabin* on the nineteenth-century Cuban novel; the well-known Italian journalist Beniamino Placido's *Due schiavitù*, a juxtaposition of Stowe's novel with Melville's "Benito Cereno" (1855); and a major reception study foundational for the present work, Orlova, *Khizhina, ustoiavshaia stoletie*.

15. The first figure is an estimate derived from Orlova, *Khizhina, ustoiavshaia stoletie*, esp. 67–98; and Orlova, *Garriet Bicher-Stou*; the second from the 1970 *Bol'shaia Sovetskaia Entsiklopediia*, ed. A. M. Prokhorov et al., 3rd ed. (Moscow: Sovetskaia Entsiklopediia, 1970), 3:403. I have raised the estimated number given in the latter source (fifty-nine editions) to account for editions appearing between 1970 and 1991, which easily bring the total to beyond seventy and probably closer to one hundred (I have by no means seen all the Soviet editions in Russian).

16. Because I will be writing often here about cut/altered Russian versions of the whole or part of *Uncle Tom's Cabin*, I want to stress at the outset that such alterations are in no way peculiar to the Russian-Soviet reception, the Wild East's reputation for "censorship" notwithstanding. As is well known, the book had been Sambo-ed, bowdlerized, and dittified virtually from its first appearance in the United States; indeed, its susceptibility to every possible variety of *détournement* seems striking enough to constitute an interesting theoretical problem in its own right. To be sure, the hybrid character of Stowe's book—incorporating sentimental melodrama, adventure stories, ghost stories, the plantation-novel genre, political argumentation, Christian sermonizing, Bible quotation, slave testimony, and elements of minstrelsy, among other sources—helped to create the possibility of such varied forms of uptake, a possibility

catalyzed by the novel's prodigious popularity and ambiguously classic-canonical status. In her discussion of *Uncle Tom*, Linda Williams eloquently expresses the problem: "How, then, shall we approach the myriad, ephemeral performances of a 'work' with no fixed text, with songs and dances that attached to certain versions and disappeared in others, over the course of eighty years, through the Civil War, the Spanish-American War, World War I, and beyond? Where do we find our text amid so many variations?" (*Playing the Race Card*, 46). See also Hedrick, *Harriet Beecher Stowe*, 213–14; M. Wood, *Blind Memory*, 143–214; Meer, *Uncle Tom Mania*; and Reynolds, *Mightier than the Sword*, 169–273. Though there were surely no "Tom shows" in Russia, adaptations for the stage did appear, and the history of Russian alterations of Stowe's novel goes back to the very first publications; as I will show, some of the most remarkable reworkings are pre-Soviet.

17. For an excellent discussion of the difficulties involved in studying "common readers," see Laura Engelstein's review essay "Print Culture." For a more general reflection on the complexities involved in the historical study of reading, see Chartier, *Order of Books*, esp. 1–24.

18. My own protocols for reception study have been influenced by Tony Bennett's notion of "reading formation," an adaptation and revision of Michel Foucault's concept of "discursive formation": "The concept of reading formation . . . is an attempt to identify the determinations that, in operating on both texts and readers, mediate the relations between text and context, connecting the two and providing the mechanism through which they productively interact in representing context, not as a set of extradiscursive relations, but as a set of intertextual and discursive relations that produce readers for texts and texts for readers. This is to question conventional conceptions of texts, readers, and contexts and separable elements, fixed in their relations to one another, by suggesting that they are variable functions within a discursively ordered set of relations. Different reading formations, that is to say, produced their own texts, their own readers, and their own contexts" ("Texts in History," 69). In the conclusion, I offer some summary remarks about the reception of *Uncle Tom's Cabin* in Russia and its enabling conditions.

19. On the small dimensions of the Russian literate public, relative to Western European societies, until after the 1860s, see Lovell, *Russian Reading Revolution*, 10.

20. I choose to speak here for the most part about "educated elites" rather than "intelligentsia(s)," not only to avoid imprecision but also due to the historical confusions and dense ideological fog that have come to obscure the latter term. As historian Boris Kolonitskij has shown in a superb revisionary essay, "intelligentsia" was used in the late nineteenth and early twentieth centuries to describe a wide variety of social categories and roles: everyone from people with higher education and members of "intellectual professions" to participants in discussion and reading circles and those who wore a certain identifiably "intellectual" garb could be tagged as *intelligenty*. Even when considered in

relation to that cluster of political beliefs associated with the classically "progressive" intelligentsia, any one or combination of those beliefs—whether they be "antibourgeois" animus, fierce advocacy of civil liberties (and opposition to the tsarist regime), religious tolerance, or revolutionary asceticism—could lead to the "intelligentsia" label being applied or self-applied. Meanwhile, the very struggle of both conservative and left-wing ideologues to avoid being identified as part of an "intelligentsia" testifies to the term's profound instability, in a context where discourse was polemically charged on all sides. Left and right alike often regarded the "intelligentsia" as foreign to both the established order and "the people," attached to ideas rather than to concrete social existence, the "common man," and so on—a charge still plainly detectable amid the squalors of contemporary anti-intellectual rhetoric—even as the far-right Union of the Russian People could seek to create an "authentically Russian intelligentsia," and Russian Marxists, a "worker's intelligentsia" (Boris I. Kolonickij, "Les identités de l'intelligentsia russe et l'anti-intellectualisme," 606, 609, 610, 614; see also Knight, "Was the Intelligentsia Part of the Nation?"). Thus I prefer to regard "intelligentsia" as a kind of symptom emerging out of social contradictions, as an ideologeme—that is, a (very real) object of discursive-political struggle—rather than as an empirical-historical category faithfully and univocally designating some circumscribable group. The great philological account remains Müller, *Intelligencija*. For a classic, deeply learned demolition of the cliché of the intelligentsia's monstrous parturition of Bolshevik tyranny, see Burbank, *Intelligentsia and Revolution*, esp. 238–55. On the other end of the spectrum, a distillation of the established, tendentious stereotypes about the intelligentsia and its wickedness can be found, purified of all nuance and undiluted by serious historical or philological research, in Morson, "What Is the Intelligentsia?"

21. That reading public will be discussed later. To be sure, the tsarist state took itself to be an enlightening force, even before the period of the Great Reforms (1860s–1870s). See Weeks, *Nation and State*; Stanislawski, *Tsar Nicholas I and the Jews*; Nathans, *Beyond the Pale*.

22. I borrow "symbolic unity" from Knight, "Was the Intelligentsia Part of the Nation?" 736.

23. Comparisons of the two nations began in the early nineteenth century: see Tocqueville's famous remarks on the "two great nations in the world which, starting from different points, seem to be advancing toward the same goal," in *Democracy in America*, 413; and Philarète Chasles's description of the bustle and flux he observed in both the United States and Russia in *Études contemporaines*, 222. See also Burbank and Cooper, *Empires in World History*, esp. 283–286.

24. On the crusading and "civilizing" mission, see Hedrick, *Harriet Beecher Stowe*, esp. 4–5, 288–89.

25. I take this phrase from the title entry for a list of "Tom show" playbills in Jorgenson, *Uncle Tom's Cabin as Book and Legend*, 31; and from Birdoff, *World's Greatest Hit*.

Chapter 1. Before Emancipation

1. See in particular David Moon's *Abolition of Serfdom in Russia*, which argues that the process begins with the abolition of mandatory state service for the nobility in 1762 and ends with the writing-off by Nicholas II of all the freed serfs' outstanding "redemption payments" in 1907 (3–4). On serfdom as a form of slavery, and on its differences from and similarities to American slavery, see Peter Kolchin's now classic study *Unfree Labor*, esp. 41–46.

2. On private publishing and preliminary censorship, both of which effectively began in Russia in the late eighteenth century, see Ruud, *Fighting Words*; Skabichevskij, *Ocherki istorii russkoj tsenzury*; and Lemke, *Ocherki*, esp. 1–182. Censorship in Russia during the years 1848–55—the last years of the reign of Tsar Nicholas I, and in the midst of which *Uncle Tom's Cabin* originally appeared in English—was notoriously repressive, and the period is known as the "epoch of censorship terror" (Lemke, *Ocherki*, 185).

3. The most famous example (about which more later) is Ivan Turgenev's *Sketches from a Hunter's Notebook*, published in *The Contemporary* between 1847 and 1851. Daniel Field writes that although "there was a relaxation of the censorship in comparison with the last years of Nicholas's reign," "this striking contrast may obscure the continuity of censorship policy and divert attention from the restrictions that were imposed on the press with regard to the peasant reform" (*End of Serfdom*, 149).

4. To take samples from only the two journals that later were the first to publish Stowe's novel: the center-liberal *Russian Messenger* (*Russkij Vestnik*) ran an important series of articles in 1856 by the famous liberal historian Boris Chicherin on the peasant community; an article in March 1857 by "V. Ch." on "Agriculture in Russia"; V. P. Bezobrazov's "Aristocracy and the Interests of the Nobility: Ideas and Observations on the Peasant Question" (September 1859); and a scathing antiserfdom piece by "P.E." on "Landowners and Peasants" (February 1859; see my discussion of "P.E.'s" article). For its part, the liberal *The Contemporary* (*Sovremennik*) published several important pieces in 1858 (clearly the *annus mirabilis* for discussion of serfdom in the press), including two series— "The Organization of the Way of Life of Serf Peasants" and "On the New Conditions of Village Life"—and Evgenij Karnovich's "Notes toward a History of Serfdom in Russia." Numerous other articles appearing during this time (like the translation of Gustave de Molinari's "On Free Labor" (*Russian Messenger*, April 1860) touch on closely affiliated issues, but the number of articles directly related to Russian serfdom is not great. As Charles Ruud has noted, however, despite the relatively small number of journals in Russia, "by the close of [Tsar Nicholas I's] reign . . . the circulation of the leading Russian journals were not widely at variance with the leading intellectual reviews in the West," which suggests that these articles did receive serious attention from educated readers (*Fighting Words*, 94).

5. I derive these figures mainly from the extensive "Bibliographical References" (based largely on holdings in the British Museum) included in the Russian translation by Zhuravskaia, *Khizhina diadi Toma* (1898), 521–32. Some of the translations are apparently abridgements, and the list does not claim to be comprehensive. On the French translations and responses, see Lucas, *La littérature anti-esclavagiste au dix-neuvième siècle*, esp. 65–67; on the German, Maclean, *Uncle Tom's Cabin in Germany*, 23–26.

6. See Orlova, *Khizhina*, 68.

7. Evidently, the very earliest mention of the book in Russia was a brief, derisive 1855 remark in an anonymous survey of contemporary American poetry in the popular journal *Biblioteka dlia chteniia*—"If, finally, the time arrives when America will properly take up the pen, it will be capable of giving the universe something better than *Uncle Tom*"—the first in a long series of Russian dismissals of Stowe as a literary artist (*Biblioteka dlia chteniia*, July 1855 [vol. 132, sec. 7]: 20); cited in Nikoliukin, *Literaturnye sviazi Rossii i SSha*, 383.

8. On Sand's response to Stowe, see Lucas, *La littérature anti-esclavagiste au dix-neuvième siècle*, 105–29.

9. For other evidence of a ban, see Orlova, *Khizhina*, 68. The establishment of diplomatic relations between Russia and the United States in 1808–9 apparently stimulated some reciprocal cultural curiosity. The main US authors known in Russia prior to Stowe were Hawthorne (whose *House of Seven Gables* appeared in translation in 1852), Irving, and above all (from the 1820s) Cooper, whose popularity in Russia, considerable to this day, was catalyzed at the time by strong interest in Sir Walter Scott and the historical novel, or more specifically novels about nation-formation; see Nikoliukin, *Literturnye sviazi Rossii i SSha*, 118, 372–75.

10. For anticipation of the abolition of serfdom, see Moon, *Abolition of Serfdom in Russia*, 61.

11. Quoted in Saul, *Distant Friends*, 302–3.

12. For more direct evidence of the mood of the censorship organs in 1857–58, see Skabichevskij, *Ocherki istorii russkoj tsenzury*, esp. 416–26.

13. On Brazil and Cuba, see Reynolds, *Mightier than the Sword*, 176.

14. It is worth noting that Secretary Lewis Cass (1782–1866), an early political ally of John C. Calhoun, was himself a moderate defender of slavery, though not a southerner. As senator from Michigan during the secession crisis, Cass often attacked abolitionist agitators on the Senate floor, speaking in the following terms on 12 May 1856: "The world had been inundated with log-cabin books about as worthy of credit as the travels of the renowned Gulliver, too often drawing their conclusions from the dictates of a wild or false heart, or of a disordered head" (quoted in Klunder, *Lewis Cass and the Politics of Moderation*, 285). Presumably, Cass would have understood some of the worries of his Russian counterparts. On southern antagonism to the book and its adaptations, see Gossett, *Uncle Tom's Cabin and American Culture*, 185–211; Hedrick, *Harriet*

Beecher Stowe, 231-32; Reynolds, *Mightier than the Sword*, 150-51, and L. Williams, *Playing the Race Card*, 83.

15. Fluency in French was a standard attainment of the Russian educated classes by the beginning of the nineteenth century.

16. Orlova, *Khizhina*, 67. On the serialization in the newspaper *Presse*, see Lucas, *La littérature anti-esclavagiste au dix-neuvième siècle*, 65.

17. Orlova, *Khizhina*, 67.

18. Ibid., 77; Tolstoj, *Polnoe sobranie sochinenij*, 47:24.

19. Pushchin, *Sochineniia i pis'ma*, 2:99. The Decembrists (who were comprised of several disparate factions in and around St. Petersburg, Moscow, and Kiev) staged an abortive revolt on 14 December 1825 through which they had hoped to overthrow the autocracy and establish either a republic or a constitutional monarchy.

20. An Old Believer is one of those Russian Orthodox believers, sometimes called *raskol'niki*, who retain the liturgical forms in use prior to the reforms instigated by Patriarch Nikon of Moscow (1652-58).

21. Cited in Orlova, *Khizhina*, 79-80.

22. N. Tourgueneff [Turgenev], "Russia and the Russians." The quote from Chapman is from her brief introduction on page 210.

23. Ibid., 218-19, extended quote from 218.

24. I have been unable to determine which "Russian comedy" Turgenev is referring to here, but he might have in mind the cruel Mrs. Prostakova in Denis Fonvizin's *The Minor* (*Nedorosl'*, 1782); my thanks to Laurence Senelick for pointing out this possible reference. The comment about the hypocritically "sad" noblewoman recalls a very similar description in one of the few extant serf narratives, M. E. Vasilieva's "Notes of a Serf-Woman" (1911), in my *Four Russian Serf Narratives*, 210-11.

25. N. Turgenev [Tourgueneff], "Russia and the Russians," 223-24.

26. Turgenev once compared a constitutional monarch to a god ruling with divine laws, in contrast to an autocrat, who was more like a shepherd ruling the herd with dogs. On his political/legal views, see Shebunin, *Nikolaj Ivanovich Turgenev*, esp. 50-51.

27. See Semevskij, *Krest'ianskji vopros*, 2:397-401. Khomyakov died of cholera after trying to treat a serf peasant ill with the disease during an epidemic.

28. Khomyakov, *Polnoe sobranie sochinenij*, 8:393.

29. Semevskij, *Krest'ianskij vopros*, 390. Semevskij notes that in fact Swedish warlords had introduced legal protections for Baltic peasants, protections removed by the Russians once they took control of the area.

30. On the question of the peasant community's antiquity, see Blum, *Lord and Peasant*, 508-15.

31. On the relation of both slavery and serfdom to "the geographic and economic expansion of Europe in the sixteenth and seventeenth centuries," see

Kolchin, *Unfree Labor*, 1–17. On rural colonization involving the state peasantry, see Sunderland, "Peasants on the Move"; and for a broad historical view, Christian, "Inner Eurasia," esp. 199–207.

32. Kolchin, *Unfree Labor*, 45.

33. Khomyakov was a confirmed Anglophile: he had traveled to England in 1847 and saw the country as a refuge of natural feeling and hospitality, mocking those who saw it as populated by nothing but "Dombeys" (i.e., by materialistic bourgeois like Paul Dombey Sr. in Dickens's novel, published in Russian in 1847–48, even as it was first appearing in English). See Katarskij, *Dikkens v Rossii*, 134–35.

34. Khomyakov, *Polnoe sobranie sochinenij*, 8:393.

35. The famous "Oblomov's Dream" section of the novel had already appeared (in 1849).

36. Khomyakov, *Polnoe sobranie sochinenij*, 8:393.

37. On this question, see Tompkins's "Sentimental Power."

38. Dickens, an avowed influence on Stowe, had been popular since the early 1840s; see Katarskij, *Dikkens v Rossii*, 79–249.

39. Zorine and Nemzer, "Les paradoxes de la sentimentalité," 95.

40. Stowe, *Uncle Tom's Cabin* (1998), 384. All further references to the English original will be to this edition, with page numbers following in parentheses (e.g., Stowe, 384). For an excellent discussion of Stowe in the context of English-language sentimentalism, see Fisher, *Hard Facts*, 91–122. To be sure, readerly preparation in modes other than the sentimental would have been important as well, especially given *Uncle Tom*'s hybrid character. In France, for instance, earlier popular fictions about slavery like Victor Hugo's slave revolt novel *Bug-Jargal* (1826) and Madame de Duras's *Ourika* (1823) paved the way for the reception of Stowe's book (Lucas, *La littérature anti-esclavagiste au dix-neuvième siècle*, 15–21), and may well have been known by Russian readers as well.

41. "Vnutrennie partii v Soedinennykh shtatakh," 12.

42. It is also worth noting that one of his main "historical sources" for the article is none other than Nikolai Turgenev's *La Russie et les Russes*, which was surely also lying on his desk at the time.

43. Aleksandr Gertsen, "Russian Serfdom," in *Sobranie sochinenij v tridtsati tomakh*, 12:7. The piece was first published in the London journal *The Leader* (nos. 189–91), on 5, 12, and 19 November 1853.

44. Gertsen, "Russian Serfdom," 33.

45. Meer, *Uncle Tom Mania*, 202. This stance became more ironic, of course, with Britain's adoption of an officially "neutral" stance (while flirting with recognizing the Confederacy) during the US Civil War. Stowe herself surely complicated this appropriation with St. Clare's remarks on the condition of the English working class, namely, his insistence that "there is no denying [St. Clare's brother] Alfred, when he says that his slaves are better off than a large

class of the population of England" (200). As Denise Kohn, Sarah Meer, and Emily B. Todd have noted, "British prefaces interpreted Stowe's novel in national terms. By the mid-nineteenth century there was a thriving discourse of British commentary on American institutions, which often stressed the contradiction of the coexistence of American ideals of freedom and liberty with slavery. . . . Prefaces to British editions of *Uncle Tom's Cabin* do not linger on the novel's emotional effects or highlight Little Eva's death, the separation of slave families, or Tom's martyrdom. Instead, *Uncle Tom's Cabin* in its British context is framed by discussions of American failings and backwardness and English superiority and progress." They add that these "British readings of *Uncle Tom's Cabin* as a reflection on American shortcomings caused a great deal of anxiety [in the United States]" ("Reading Stowe as a Transatlantic Writer," in Kohn, Meer, and Todd, *Transatlantic Stowe*, xix–xxi).

46. P.E., "Pomeshchiki i krest'iane," 225. The essay is dated December 1858, and a footnote on 225 indicates that it was published with "omissions."

47. For "Tom" showbiz, see Meer, *Uncle Tom Mania*, 134.

48. Compare, for instance, Eric Sundquist's argument that "sentiment, not antislavery made the book popular," with Linda Williams's insistence that "what was new in Stowe's novel were . . . not the tears of the powerless . . . but the use of tears to cross racial barriers, to create new pictures of interracial unity and emotional intimacy" (Sundquist, "Slavery, Revolution, and the American Renaissance," 18; Williams, *Playing the Race Card*, 54–55). See also Eric Lott's remarks on the Irish American press's criticisms of "the hypocritical antislavery Stowe" in *Love and Theft*, 299. For an excellent overview of twentieth-century American grapplings with these aspects of Stowe, see Warren, "Afterlife of *Uncle Tom's Cabin*."

49. Gertsen, "Russian Serfdom," 7.

50. Gertsen, *Sobranie sochinenij v tridtsati tomakh*, 12:509. For a highly entertaining account of Golovin's literary and political escapades, see Lemke, *Nikolaevskie zhandarmy i literatura*, 555–72. Lemke presents Golovin's planned "Tom" as pure opportunism, an attempt to cash in on the slavery theme.

51. This information comes from Lemke, "Emigrant Ivan Golovin." From what I can gather, no trace remains of the manuscript.

52. Golovin is probably referring to the "Essai politique sur l'île de Cuba," first published in 1808 in the series *Voyages au regions équinoxiales du Nouveau Continent, fait en 1799, 1800, 1801, 1802, 1803 et 1804* (published between 1805 and 1834). Golovin's chapter "A Trip to Cuba" in his *Stars and Stripes or American Impressions* is dated "Havannah [*sic*], April 1856" (228). The same book contains a chapter titled "American Slavery and Russian Serfdom" but no mention of *Uncle Tom*.

53. Golovin, *Rovira*, 31.

54. Ibid., 5–9 (not numbered). Humboldt, the great geographer and naturalist of Latin America, had traveled extensively through Russia in 1829. For his antislavery views and his work on Cuba, see Cuevas Diaz, "Presencia de Alejandro de Humboldt."

55. The review appeared in "Zagranichnye izvestiia."

56. Field, *End of Serfdom*, 83.

57. In Nikoliukin, *Russian Discovery of America*, 213. The letter was first published in Russian in *Vestnik Evropy* 12 (1903): 637–39. Nekrasov published a number of major American works over the course of the 1850s, including *The House of the Seven Gables*, *The Scarlet Letter*, and *The Song of Hiawatha*.

58. The six translators were Messrs. Tol', Novosil'skij, Kalistov, Borshchov, Pashkovskij, and Butuzov; it seems that the bulk of the work was done by the last three. See "Gonorarnye vedomosti *Sovremennika*," in Reiser et al., *Literaturnoe nasledstvo*, 3:245. For Novosil'skij, see Orlova, *Khizhina*, 75. I have not examined the *Son of the Fatherland* excerpts in detail.

59. See Reiser et al., *Literaturnoe Nasledstvo*, 3:279–80; Foote, *St. Petersburg Censorship Committee*, 49–50; and Orlova, *Khizhina*, 76.

60. Pushchin, *Sochineniia i pis'ma*, 352–53.

61. I base this on the claim made by the publisher D. D. Fedorov in his preface to the edition he put out in 1883 (Bicher-Stou, *Khizhina diadi Toma ili zhizn' sredi rabov*) that this was in fact the first translation based entirely on Stowe's original text. Fedorov, the son of publisher D. F. Fedorov, who had published a version of the novel based on the *Contemporary* translation in 1871 (Bicher-Stou, *Khizhina diadi Toma*), was a man of the book trade and no doubt familiar with several earlier editions of *Uncle Tom*.

62. Cf. "Khizhina diadi Toma," *Russkij Vestnik* 13, no. 2 (February 1858), 304. "Serfs" is translated properly as *krepostnye*.

63. Specifically, from "The nobles in Louis XVI's time" to Alfred's "Stuff!—nonsense!" (Stowe, 276–77).

64. Bicher-Stou, *Khizhina diadi Toma* (1858), 336.

65. Stowe, *La Cabane de l'Oncle Tom ou les Noirs en Amérique*, 313. The *Messenger* version seems to be based on another translation that I have yet to identify. Edith Lucas notes that the translations by Léon Pilatte (1852), Louis Enault (1853), Madame Belloc (1853), and Louis Barré (1853) were among the most exact, so the *Messenger Tom* might have been derived from one of those (Lucas, *La littérature anti-esclavagiste au dix-neuvième siècle*, 77–90).

66. A full investigation of the problem would of course involve looking through all eleven of the early French translations, which I have not done. Nor is it easy to say whether the Russians knew that they were working with an already-censored text; if they did, this knowledge surely did not extend to awareness of specific alterations. See Lucas, *La littérature anti-esclavagiste au dix-neuvième siècle*, 239–40; and Goldstein, "Fighting French Censorship," esp. 787–88.

67. Apart from the shift from "canaille" to "Negroes," the diction of the Russian passage shows that it is based on the same Wailly-Texier French version (*La Cabane de l'Oncle Tom ou les Noirs en Amérique*).

Chapter 2. After Serfdom, before October

1. Quoted in Skabichevskij, *Ocherki po istorii russkoj tsenzury*, 418–19. The memo is dated 27 December 1857.

2. See Moon, *Abolition of Serfdom in Russia*, 88–97.

3. Indeed, some early British commentators charged Stowe with "undue leniency to slaveholders" (Meer, *Uncle Tom Mania*, 134).

4. Nikolaj Chernyshevskij, "Otvet na zamechaniia g. Provintsiala," in *Polnoe sobranie sochinenij*, 148. In fact, Chernyshevsky's reply appeared in the *Contemporary* (*Sovremennik* 3 [1858]: 104-13) without these and several more pages of comments (they were added later by the editors of the complete works), but it seems that they were excised for reasons of space. He also makes brief mention of Stowe for more or less rhetorical purposes (in the context of a defense of women's equality) in his famous *What Is to Be Done?*, 348.

5. Quoted in Orlova, *Khizhina*, 82.

6. See esp. "Thinking Proletariat" in Pisarev, *Selected Philosophical, Social and Political Essays*, 635–46.

7. In "Plato's Idealism," in Pisarev, *Selected Philosophical, Social and Political Essays*, 79.

8. I. Turgenev, *Memoires d'un Seigneur Russe*. Chronologically, Turgenev seems to have been the third Russian, after Lermontov and Gogol, to be discovered in the West European world; see Dorothy Brewster's endlessly fascinating *East-West Passage*.

9. The stories published (in whole or in part) were "Khor and Kalinych," "Singers," "Two Landowners," "My Neighbor Radilov," "Bailiff," "Village Doctor," "Meeting," "The Hamlet of the Shchigrovskii Region," and "Bezhin Meadow." The following year, selections from Turgenev's *Sketches* also appeared in Charles Dickens's journal *Household Words* (2 March, 31 March, 21 April, and 24 November 1855). This was the period of the Crimean War (1853-56) and thus of heightened English interest in Russia; the same issue of *Fraser's* contained a long, detailed description (complete with charts) of the structure of the Russian army.

10. I. Turgenev [Ivan Tourghenief], "Photographs from Russian Life," 209.

11. Ibid., 210-11.

12. James's key statement is in his early article (written before he met Turgenev) "Ivan Turgéniew." "It was . . . in thoroughly genial, poetical portraiture, that [Turgenev] first made his mark. 'The Memoirs of a Sportsman' were published in 1852, and were considered, says one of the two French translators of the work, much the same sort of contribution to the question of Russian

serfdom as Mrs. Stowe's famous novel to that of American slavery. This, perhaps, is forcing a point, for M. [Turgenev's] group of tales strikes us much less as a passionate *pièce de circonstance* than as a disinterested work of art. But circumstances helped it, of course, and it made a great impression,—an impression which testifies to no small culture on the part of Russian readers. For never, surely, was a work with a polemic bearing more consistently low in tone, as painters say. The author treats us to such a scanty dose of flagrant horrors that the moral of the book is obvious only to attentive readers. No single episode pleads conclusively against the 'peculiar institution' of Russia; the lesson is in the cumulative testimony of a multitude of fine touches,—in an after-sense of sadness which sets wise readers thinking" (333).

13. Buell, "Harriet Beecher Stowe," 190.

14. "Sur le roman rural en Russie," in Herzen, *Sobranie sochinenij v tridtsati tomakh*, 453–60. The essay was actually written as a letter to the German translator (M. Meysenbug) of another antiserfdom work, D. Grigorovich's *The Fisherman*.

15. Ibid., 459.

16. For the *Sketches'* polemical role, see Moon, *Abolition of Serfdom in Russia*, 30–31. Moon is no doubt correct in denying that Turgenev's book had a significant effect on government opinion, although I believe he understates its intense and thoroughgoing (if, relative to Stowe, inexplicit) animus against serfdom. English-language prefaces also made such comparisons with *Uncle Tom's Cabin*. Indeed, the title of Stowe's book became a figure for "protest novel" as such by the early twentieth century: a translation of Leonid Andreev's famous story "Red Laughter" (1905), a shattering depiction of the horrors of the Russo-Japanese War, appeared in the *New York Times* with the headline "A Russian 'Uncle Tom's Cabin' That Has Created a Sensation throughout the Empire," and prefaced by a lead paragraph beginning, "Since 'Uncle Tom's Cabin' was written no book has so powerfully stirred a nation's heart as did 'The Crimson Laughter' of [Andreev]" ("'Crimson Laughter' Terrified the Czar"). See my later discussion of Tolstoy.

17. For Turgenev's "Hannibal's oath" taken against serfdom, see Blum, *Lord and Peasant in Russia*, 568.

18. In I. Turgenev, *Polnoe sobranie pisem v trinadtsati tomakh*, 3:52. Apart from this meeting with Turgenev and another apparently apocryphal Turgenev anecdote (discussed later), we know little about Stowe's own connections with Russia and Russians. Apparently she learned from one General Taylor that the Russian writer Olga Alekseevna Novikova (1840–1925) was one of her admirers. Stowe wrote Novikova a letter (26 June 1869) in which she expressed pleasure in knowing that there were people in Russia "who read in our own English language and sympathize with us" (reported in Orlova, *Khizhina*, 88). In later years Novikova, who lived most of her life in London, devoted much of her time to defending "Slavism" and the most reactionary policies of the tsarist

regime before the court of British opinion, publishing as "Madame Olga Novikoff."

19. Ivan Turgenev, "The Inn," in *Three Novellas*, 87–148; here 147.

20. Reported in Mainwaring's introduction to *Three Novellas*, 3.

21. I. Turgenev, *Polnoe sobranie pisem*, 2:144 and 492; I. Turgenev, *Polnoe sobranie sochineniia v dvadtsati tomakh*, 2:606–9.

22. I. Turgenev, *Polnoe sobranie pisem*, 144. See also Kaspin, "*Uncle Tom's Cabin.*"

23. I. Turgenev, *Polnoe sobranie sochinenij*, 4:147.

24. "Smoke" in I. Turgenieff [*sic*], *Spring Freshets, Smoke and Other Stories*, 27.

25. On this reproach, see chapter 1, note 7.

26. Andreevskij, *Entsiklopedicheskii Slovar'* [Brockhaus-Efron], 4:19.

27. The phrase "puritan protest" comes from an article on Stowe in the *Literary Encyclopedia* of 1930 (to be discussed later). The article also remarks that Stowe's exposure of the intimate details of Byron's life is characterized by "particular hypocrisy" (Friche, *Literaturnaia Entsiklopediia*, 1:501–3).

28. Tolstoy, "What Is Art?," 22:299.

29. It is often forgotten that *Uncle Tom's Cabin* is the first book on record to be proposed as "the great American novel" (by John W. DeForest, in 1868). For a superb essay on Stowe as novelist, see Buell, "Harriet Beecher Stowe."

30. "What Is Art?," 283. See also 285–88.

31. Tolstoj, *Perepiska s russkimi pisateliami*, 2:103.

32. It is worth noting here that in later years Fet, having become a very wealthy landowner, began thinking and writing about contemporary agricultural practices and economics in a rather laissez-faire spirit, adding in many of his own observations of peasant society; see Fet, "Nashi Korni."

33. Tolstoj, *Perepiska s russkimi pisateliami*, 1:362. Interestingly, Turgenev had recently praised "Polikushka" in a letter to Fet as evidence of Tolstoy's increasing mastery of fiction.

34. For Fet's more literature-specific thoughts on the "immutability" of the "laws of art," see S. Balukhatyi et al., *Russkie pisateli o literature*, 1:432–455.

35. Tolstoj, *Perepiska s russkimi pisateliami*, 1:364.

36. Ibid., 385. The letter was written 15 June 1867.

37. Ibid., 387 (reply of 28 June 1867).

38. Tol'stoi, *Polnoe sobranie sochinenij*, 66:58.

39. Ibid., 52:131. Varvara (Barbara) Nikolaevna MacGahan (1852–1904; born Elagina) was the daughter of one of Tolstoy's old friends and widow of the American journalist Januarius MacGahan (1844–78), famous for his reportage on the Russo-Turkish War. Varvara MacGahan was a journalist as well and wrote a novel in English, *Xenia Repnina: A Story of Russia To-day* (1890). On the MacGahans, see Saul, *Concord and Conflict*, 96, 331, 358, 369–70.

40. In Anisimov et al., *Tolstoj i zarubezhnyj mir*, 1:428. George corresponded with and revered Tolstoy.

41. Twelve issues of the journal appeared in 1862–63. For a good overview of the journal's history, see Smirnov, *"Iasnaia Poliana" L'va Tolstogo*.

42. It was republished later as *Diadia Tom, ili zhizn' negrov-rabov v Amerike*.

43. Ibid., 10; see also Orlova, *Khizhina*, 83.

44. Bicher-Stou, *Khizhina diadi Toma* (1917). See also the Sytin editions from 1894 and 1916.

45. Quoted in Orlova, *Khizhina*, 84.

46. Ibid.

47. Ibid.

48. This trend prevailed, even as the book came to be read, at least from the early 1880s onward, mainly in Russian, even by members of the educated elites (except for a relatively small contingent fluent in English).

49. In those other countries, at least the English-speaking ones, the adult reception of Stowe's novel seems to have been mediated to a considerable extent through the theatrical versions (although parents would have encountered prose versions for children as well). N. V. Chekhov's 1909 study of children's literature in Russia indicates that many of the classic works by foreign authors read by children—novels and stories by Alphonse Daudet, Jules Verne, Charles Dickens, George Eliot, and Stowe among others—had already been packaged as writing for children in their home countries (*Detskaia literatura*, 157–71). See also Hochman, *Uncle Tom's Cabin*, esp. 142–43, 208–30.

50. N. V. Chekhov, *Detskaia literatura*, 27–52. Chekhov (no relation to Anton) describes Stowe as the second American writer, after Cooper, to become a significant children's writer in Russia: "In the 1850s, what was then the most burning topic of American life—the problem of the liberation of black slaves—elicited the appearance of a book that, notwithstanding its weak literary merits, circumnavigated the whole world with surprising speed, everywhere making an enormous impression and doing everything that a single book could do to further the freeing of the slaves in America. . . . [*Uncle Tom's Cabin*] was destined first to play a huge role in the lives of adults, and then (once its work was done in that area) pass over into the sphere of children's literature and become one of its prized possessions. We make no mistake if we prophesy for that book the same or perhaps an even longer life within children's literature than *Robinson Crusoe* has enjoyed. In truth, this book made black Negroes—beaten down, disadvantaged, and humiliated—the intimates of all thinking humanity, and gave them millions of brothers and friends among the younger generation. The role of this book in children's literature is hardly smaller than its role as a political pamphlet in North America in the 1850s" (162–63). See also Karajchentseva, *Russkaia detskaia kniga XVIII-XX vv.*, esp. 165.

51. Quoted in N. V. Chekhov, *Detskaia literatura*, 5. Chekhov does argue that Belinsky's words "became as it were a manifesto for the idealistic direction of our children's literature" (6).

52. "Tom's mythic stature derives in part from his seeming ability, from

one moment to the next, to be any age. He ranges from being a 'sort of patriarch in religious matters' . . . to 'simple and childlike' . . . to 'uncle' and biological and spiritual father: Cassy calls him 'Father Tom.' . . . It is only on his deathbed that he talks about 'this poor old body'" (Alessandro Portelli, "*Uncle Tom's Cabin* (Harriet Beecher Stowe, United States, 1852)" in Franco Moretti, ed., *The Novel, Volume I: History, Geography, and Culture*, 805–6.

53. On the beginnings of children's literature in Russia, see Kudriavtseva, *Dlia serdtsa i razuma*. On responses to the new readerships, N. V. Chekhov, *Detskaia literatura*, 53; and A. I. Rejtblat's bibliography in his *Ot Bovy k Bal'montu*, 212–32.

54. See Rogger, *Russia*, 85.

55. On the inadequacy of migration to the towns as a "safety valve," see Acton, *Russia*, 103. On the impact of increasing literacy, see Rejtblat, *Ot Bovy k Bal'montu*, esp. 15–72, 277–93; and Jeffrey Brooks, *When Russia Learned to Read*, esp. 295–352.

56. See Rejtblat, *Ot Bovy k Bal'montu*, 66.

57. Lucas specifically aligns the *Uncle Tom* reception with the thought of Felicité Lammenais (1782–1854) and his followers (*La littérature anti-esclavagiste au dix-neuvième siècle*, 241–44).

58. Rejtblat, *Ot Bovy k Bal'montu*, 34, 286–88. The term "vanishing mediator" comes from Jameson, "Vanishing Mediator; or, Max Weber as Storyteller." We might compare this mediating function with that of "Tom shows" in the United States, which helped to make the previously disreputable space of the theater acceptable to "decent folk"; see Jo-Ann Morgan, *Uncle Tom's Cabin as Visual Culture*, 88.

59. See, for instance, Bicher-Stou, *Khizhina diadi Toma ili belye i chernye* (1895).

60. On its appeal to radicals, see Reynolds, *Mightier than the Sword*, 175.

61. See Brooks, *When Russia Learned to Read*, 337–41.

62. Bicher-Stou, *Khizhina diadi Toma, ili belye i chernye* (1884).

63. These notions involved a critique of the traditional authoritarian regimentation of school-based learning in Russia and advocacy of expanding the range of student choice while minimizing coercion. See Kelly, *Children's World*, 32–35.

64. Bicher-Stou, *Khizhina diadi Toma*, 417–18.

65. Ibid., 447.

66. Ibid., 418–19.

67. Bicher-Stou, *Khizhina diadi Toma ili kak negry zhili v nevole* (1903), 24. This 1903 *Yasnaya Polyana* edition, almost lacking paragraph breaks, is very short, cheaply printed, and pedagogically oriented, with an additional historical contextualization added at the beginning (3–4).

68. "Though a child, [Eva] was a beautiful reader,—a fine musical ear, a quick poetic fancy, and an instinctive sympathy with what is grand and noble,

made her such a reader of the Bible as Tom had never before heard. At first, she read to please her humble friend; but soon her own earnest nature threw out its tendrils, and wound itself around the majestic book; and Eva loved it, because it woke in her strange yearnings, and strong, dim emotions, such as impassioned, imaginative children love to feel" (Stowe, 267). See also Morgan, *Uncle Tom's Cabin as Visual Culture*, 28–29.

69. For Russian examples, see above all Tolstoj, *Azbuka*, but also Ushinskij, *Pedagogicheskie sochineniia v shesti tomakh*, esp. vol. 3; Korf, *Nash drug*. On the US side, see the AMS reprint series edited by Robert C. Morris, *Freedmen's Schools and Textbooks*. See also Morris, *Reading, 'Riting, and Reconstruction*; Hartman, *Scenes of Subjection*, esp. 115–63; and H. A. Williams, *Self-Taught*.

70. Frierson, *Peasant Icons*, 17.

71. Bicher-Stou, *Khizhina diadi Toma* (1902), 374.

72. Primary iconographic sources appear to have been provided by Stowe, *Uncle Tom's Cabin* (1904); *Uncle Tom's Cabin* (n.d.), and no doubt other editions as well. As Marcus Wood has shown, most American and British editions of *Uncle Tom's Cabin* were accompanied by illustrations that helped both to frame interpretation and to focus attention on a limited number of "scenes." This repertoire of *Tom* tableaux, about fifteen in number, was basically set by George Cruikshank's early engravings for the book (Wood, *Blind Memory*, 151). As Wood writes, *Uncle Tom's Cabin* is "the key site for the examination of what popular audiences in the mid-nineteenth century wanted to see as, and what publishers wanted to impose upon, the representation of blacks within slave systems" (143); in Russia, to be sure, some of the more violent and sexual *Tom* visual topoi—the scene of Rosa's whipping, for instance, not described in the book but often illustrated—are almost entirely avoided. (On *Tom* illustrations, see also Morgan, *Uncle Tom's Cabin as Visual Culture*.) For their part, late nineteenth-early twentieth Russian norms for visually representing black people have been insufficiently studied. The conflicts generated among mid-nineteenth-century Russian radical thinkers by their simultaneous commitment to Darwin-influenced evolutionary science and to egalitarianism (Pisarev was caught in this dilemma early on) are well outlined in Rogers, "Racism and Russian Revolutionists." Some venues for depictions and theorizations of various "races," such as the *Russian Anthropological Journal* (1900–1916 and 1922–1930) were primarily devoted to studies of peoples living within the Russian Empire. Inquiries into the origins and physical characteristics of the most famous Russian poet, Alexander Pushkin—whose great-grandfather, Ibrahim Hannibal, was a black African—were exceptions: one, a study by the physical anthropologist Dmitri Anuchin, maintained that Pushkin's racial background was "Ethiopian" rather than "Negroid," the latter category of person being incapable, in Anuchin's view, of creating "culture" (Anuchin, *A. S. Pushkin*). On this topic, see Nepomnyashchy, Svobodny, and Trigos, *Under the Sky of My Africa*; and especially Mogil'ner, *Homo Imperii*, 216–36. How visual stereotypes

related to everyday practice is another matter. US blacks did in fact move to Russia, and some found enormous success there, particularly as entrepreneurs in the entertainment industry; see Saul, *Concord and Conflict*, 562; Blakely, *Russia and the Negro*, 39–70; and Alexandrov, *The Black Russian*.

73. Wood, *Blind Memory*, 176. Stowe's text provides the motivation, of course ("He leaned over the back of the chair, and covered his face with his large hands" [44]). Perhaps some of the terrifying power of the silhouettes of scenes from slavery times created by contemporary African American artist Kara Walker derives from the way the flat, black surface of the silhouettes directly evokes this historical problem of "nonrepresentability." One of Walker's best known works in this mode is titled *The End of Uncle Tom and the Grand Allegorical Tableau of Eva in Heaven* (1995).

74. A perfect example would be Page's "Ole 'Stracted," in his *In Ole Virginia*, 140–61.

75. On the mortgage melodrama, see Roach, *Cities of the Dead*, 179–238.

76. Bicher-Stou, *Khizhina diadi Toma* (1902), 450–51.

77. Reported in Blakely, *Russia and the Negro*, 94.

78. Bicher-Stou, *Khizhina diadi Toma* (1902), 452–55.

79. "[After 1893], *Uncle Tom's Cabin* became a product, clothed in different packagings, recycled in all kinds of ways, and used to advertise other consumer goods. The devaluation of the novel, through cheap editions, Tom shows, the use of distorted images in advertising—which must be understood within the context of the degraded image of African Americans at the time—certainly played no inconsiderable role in the negative critical assessment of the work that was to follow" (Parfait, *Publishing History of Uncle Tom's Cabin*, 175).

80. Morgan, *Uncle Tom's Cabin as Visual Culture*, 18. See also Parfait, *Publishing History of Uncle Tom's Cabin*, 152.

81. See Meer, *Uncle Tom Mania*, 253–56; Reynolds, *Mightier than the Sword*, 213–31. As Reynolds shows, part of the US struggle over the meanings of race and the Civil War during these years happened onscreen, as can be seen by juxtaposing D. W. Griffith's notorious and influential *Birth of a Nation* (1915; based on Dixon's *The Clansman* [1904]) with William Robert Daly's 1914 *Uncle Tom's Cabin*, where Tom was actually played by an African American; see *Mightier than the Sword*, 218–233. Barbara Hochman makes the superb point that "*Uncle Tom's Cabin* was an extremely important book for African-American readers in the years between the court decision *Plessy vs. Ferguson* (1896), which made segregation legal, and *Brown vs. Board of Education* (1954), which reversed that decision. In the intervening years, when many young African Americans were the children or grandchildren of ex-slaves, information about slavery was paradoxically scarce. In the public sphere, slave narratives 'virtually disappeared from American cultural memory for over a century' [quoting W. J. T. Mitchell, *Picture Theory: Verbal and Visual Representation* (Chicago: University of Chicago

Press, 1995), 189]. Ex-slaves themselves, eager to move on, were reluctant to hand down stories of their experience to their children. In this context *Uncle Tom's Cabin* was an eye-opener for young black readers who were hungry for information about their family's past and about slavery in general" (Hochman, *Uncle Tom's Cabin*, 232; on the novel as a safe "classic" and "masterpiece," see 140–45).

82. On writing about peasant life, see Herzberg, "Onkel Vanjas Hütte"; and Herzberg and Schmidt, *Vom Wir zum Ich.*

83. For the twenty-four-page version, see Bicher-Stou, *Khizhina diadi Toma ili belye i chernye* (1910).

84. Vit translation, Bicher-Stou, *Khizhina diadi Toma* (1916), 156.

85. Bicher-Stou, *Khizhina diadi Toma* (1912), 240.

86. Here the translation follows the biblical quote as cited by Stowe.

87. Bicher-Stou, *Khizhina diadi Toma* (1908), 486, italics in original.

88. For a forceful account of the structuring presence of imperialist ideology in *Uncle Tom's Cabin*, see Elizabeth Ammons, "Freeing the Slaves and Banishing the Blacks: Racism, Empire, and Africa in *Uncle Tom's Cabin*," in Ammons, *Harriet Beecher Stowe's Uncle Tom's Cabin*, 227–47.

89. In Russian, the word "soul" could also mean "serf"—thus the joke in the title of Gogol's *Dead Souls.*

90. Bicher-Stou, *Khizhina diadi Toma* (1912), 265–67.

91. On *Tom's* use in advertising, see Parfait, *Publishing History of Uncle Tom's Cabin*, 174–75. Parfait notes (153–75) how this commercialization expanded apace especially after 1894–1896, when a number of scholarly and memorial editions appeared.

Chapter 3. The Early Soviet Period (to 1945)

1. Fitzpatrick, *Cultural Front*, 4–5. For more on the commonalities between Bolsheviks and liberals in regard to print culture and its commercialization, see Lovell, *Russian Reading Revolution*, 12. On reading culture during the early Soviet period, see Dobrenko, *Making of the State Reader.*

2. In Murakhina's afterword to the 1912 Sytin ed. (436).

3. Two were published in Odessa, four in Moscow and/or Leningrad: *Khizhina diadi Toma*, adapted for children by V. I. Pavlov (Odessa: Odespoligraf, 1925); *Khizhina diadi Toma*, adapted by E. N. Vinogradskaia (Moscow and Leningrad: Gosudarstvennoe Izdatel'stvo, 1925); *Khizhina diadi Toma* (Moscow and Leningrad: Gosudarstvennoe izdatel'stvo, 1928)—also adapted by Vinogradskaia; *Khizhina diadi Toma: Epizody iz romana*, adapted by A. Dejch (Moscow: Ogonek, 1928); *Khizhina diadi Toma*, ed. and abridged by M. Leonti'eva, 2nd ed. (Odessa: Odespoligraf, 1928); and *Begletsy: Epizody iz romana 'Khizhina diadi Toma,'* adapted by N. Moguchij (Moscow and Leningrad: Molodaia Gvardiia,

1930). The 5th edition is the first version edited by Leonti'eva, whose publication date I have not determined. See also Karajchentseva, *Russkaia detskaia kniga XVIII–XX vv.*, 218.

4. A contemporary Soviet study of the publishing scene in 1922 found that just over 1 percent of all books published in the Russian Soviet Federative Socialist Republic were for children, the lowest for any category of publication (*Pechat' RSFSR v 1922 godu*, 34, 62, and diagram 5).

5. Suny, *Soviet Experiment*, 190.

6. From what I can tell, the last complete prerevolutionary edition appeared in 1898; later editions were altered or condensed to wildly varying extents.

7. Bicher-Stou, *Khizhina diadi Toma*, adapted by E. N. Vinogradskaia (1928), 4. On African-American Communist activism in the United States during the 1930s, see Kelley, *Hammer and Hoe*.

8. Ibid., 79. Moguchij's 1930 edition, which maintains a good deal of Stowe's minstrel-influenced humor and stereotyping (e.g., many of Sam and Andy's antics; Aunt Chloe wiping her face with egg whites to keep it nice and shiny [24]), focuses overwhelmingly on the escapes of George, Eliza, and Cassy; St. Clare and Eva do not appear, and Tom vanishes after being sold halfway through.

9. Ibid., 61.

10. Bicher-Stou, *Khizhina diadi Toma*, ed. and abridged by M. Leonti'eva (1928), 26.

11. Bicher-Stou, *Khizhina diadi Toma*, adapted by E. N. Vinogradskaia (1925), 74.

12. Bicher-Stou, *Khizhina diadi Toma*, ed. and abridged by M. Leonti'eva (1928), 24.

13. Bicher-Stou, *Khizhina diadi Toma*, adapted by E. N. Vinogradskaia (1925), 47.

14. Bicher-Stou, *Khizhina diadi Toma*, adapted by E. N. Vinogradskaia (1928), 47.

15. Bicher-Stou, *Khizhina diadi Toma*, adapted by A. Dejch (1928), 36.

16. Bicher-Stou, *Khizhina diadi Toma*, adapted by E. N. Vinogradskaia (1928), 69.

17. Bicher-Stou, *Khizhina diadi Toma*, adapted by E. N. Vinogradskaia (1925), 15.

18. Bicher-Stou, *Khizhina diadi Toma*, ed. and abridged by M. Leonti'eva (1928), 217.

19. Ibid.

20. Ibid.

21. "According to Lenin, propaganda involved extended theoretical explanations of the socioeconomic processes that underlay surface phenomena such as unemployment. By appealing to audience members' reason, the propagandist

aimed to cultivate in them a whole new worldview. Propaganda was a process of education that required a relatively sophisticated, informed audience. Agitation, on the other hand, motivated the audience to action by appealing to their emotions with short, stark stories. The agitator did not seek to change his listeners' worldview, but to mobilize them. . . . Definitions from the first edition of *The Great Soviet Encyclopedia* link propaganda with education and agitation with organization/mobilization" (Lenoe, *Closer to the Masses*, 28).

22. Clark, "Little Heroes and Big Deeds," 193.

23. Friche et al., *Literaturnaia Entsiklopediia*, 1:501–3, here 502. The article quotes St. Clare's remark: "The slave-owner can whip his refractory slave to death,—the capitalist can starve him to death" (Stowe, 237).

24. Ibid., 503. Interestingly, Maxim Gorky, one of the fathers of Soviet children's literature, included Stowe's novel in a late (1936) list of recommended readings for Soviet youngsters; he had placed *Uncle Tom's Cabin* at the head of his list of books for children aged nine to fifteen when working as an editor in 1921 for Zinovij Grzhebin's Berlin and Petrograd-based publishing house (Gor'kij, *O detskoj literature*, 76–80, 126–128).

25. See Lovell, *Russian Reading Revolution*, 25–60; here 55.

26. On the "pilgrimages," See Blakely, *Russia and the Negro*, 80–104; and K. A. Baldwin, *Beyond the Color Line*. On anxiety about the "peasant theme," see Fitzpatrick, *Stalin's Peasants*, 128–51. To be sure, a kind of Soviet "peasant minstrelsy" emerged in the 1930s as well, in an effort to ground the new order in folk authenticity; see Miller, *Folklore for Stalin*.

27. Clark, *Soviet Novel*, 177–80.

28. Orlova, *Khizhina*, 74.

29. Ibid., 38. Orlova (1918–89), whose husband was the well-known author and dissident Lev Kopelev (1912–97), authored several works on American literature, including *Huckleberry Finn's Descendants* (1964), *Hemingway's "For Whom the Bell Tolls"* (1969), and *The Raised Sword: A Story about John Brown* (1975). She and Kopelev were compelled to leave the USSR at the end of 1980 and settled in West Germany. Her *Memoirs* were published in English in 1983.

30. On *Uncle Tom* and 1960s debates about nonviolence, see Reynolds, *Mightier than the Sword*, 260, 263, 266–67, 273.

31. In Tsvetaeva, *Selected Poems*, 122.

32. Perhaps this also helps expose the authentically apocalyptic character of the "Christ" allegory informing Stowe's representation of Tom: for Tom *not* to die, the world as such would have to be utterly different from what it now is.

33. One of her first successes was a 1925 adaptation, with director Boris Zon, of *Don Quixote*, which starred the young Nikolai Cherkasov (later famous as the titular hero of Sergei Eisenstein's *Alexander Nevsky* [1938] and *Ivan the Terrible* [1945]) as the Don; much later, he took up the role onscreen (in Grigorij Kozintsev's 1957 film). Cherkasov played a judge in the 1927 *Uncle Tom* adaptation. See A. Turkov, *Ot desiati do devianosta*, 6–14, 48; Cherkasov, *Zapiski*

sovetskogo aktera, 53; Drejden, *Nikolai Cherkasov*, 422; Liubashevskij [D. Del'], *Rasskazy o teatre i kino*, 79–82.

34. See RGALI, f. 2546, op. 1, d. 4 for Brushtein's *Uncle Tom* drafts from 1927 to 1966; and Brushtejn, "Bicher-Stou."

35. The four-act play was called *Slaves* (*Nevol'niki*), focused almost entirely on the New Orleans–St. Clare part of the story, and left both Tom and Eva alive at the end. I am not certain that it was performed; it was apparently never published in book form, and Lidin did not include it in either edition of his collected works (1928 and 1973). See RGALI, f. 3102, op. 2, d. 94. Unlike the United States and Britain, where stage versions of *Uncle Tom's Cabin* were virtually as well known as the novel, Russia became and remained acquainted with Stowe's prose narrative, however altered, first and foremost. The only nineteenth-century stage adaptation I have discovered is a rather long-winded 1890 melodrama by Mikhail Pavlovich Fedorov (1839–1900), a playwright and critic who also worked during the 1890s as editor of *New Times*, Russia's top-selling daily newspaper, when Anton Chekhov was publishing his stories in its pages. The main innovation of Fedorov's play involves compressing Legree and George Harris's master together into a single figure named Harris, who is both an ex-slave and burns with unrequited passion for Eliza: the George-Eliza-Harris drama takes up almost all of the play's action. Senator Bird is made a more heroic character—stepping in to help buy Eliza during the extended slave auction sequence, for instance—Tom is largely marginal and survives at the end, and the St. Clare portions of Stowe's novel are essentially elided (although a character named "St. Clare" does appear), as they would be in Brushtein's versions (Fedorov, *Khizhina diadi Toma*). (Fedorov's play, like most contemporary plays published in Russia at the time, was lithographed from a handwritten copy and printed in a small run exclusively for use by theaters; on this publishing practice, see Rejtblat, *Ot Bovy k Bal'montu*, 349–56.) It would seem that George L. Aiken's highly popular 1852 stage adaptation might also have been performed, though I have seen no evidence that it was.

36. Turkov, *Ot desiati do devianosta*, 14; Liubashevskij, *Rasskazy o teatre i kino*, 78. V. I. Bejer's spare, stark set design was influenced by Constructivist practice; see Briantsev, *Khudozhnik v teatre dlia detej*, esp. 37.

37. Liubashevskij, *Rasskazy o teatre i kino*, 80. I have not had the opportunity to examine a script of this first Brushtein-Zon version. It was evidently revived in 1932 at Moscow's Second Art Theater, prior to the establishment of diplomatic relations with the United States in November 1933 ("Uncle Tom in Russia," *Literary Digest* 114 [2 July 1932]: 16–17, quoted in Gossett, *Uncle Tom's Cabin and American Culture*, 287).

38. A. Brushtejn and B. V. Zon, *Chernyi Tovar* (1938), in RGALI, f. 2452, op. 3, d. 1789, here l. 50.

39. RGALI, f. 2452, op. 3, d. 1789, l. 41.

40. See, for instance, Brushtejn, *Khizhina diadi Toma: Drama A. Brushtejn po motivam proizvedenij Bicher-Stou.*

41. See *Programma*. The production was directed by E. M. Sakharov.

42. According to one source, over sixteen thousand people were repressed (executed or sent to prison or a labor camp) in 1937–38 in the Krasnoyarsk region alone; among the executed were nine musicians in the Krasnoyarsk Theater's symphony orchestra (Sirotinin, "Kommunisticheskij terror v Krasnoiarskom krae"). Among the many works on the terror, Getty and Naumov's *Road to Terror* is a standout. In an article on the history of internationalism, Perry Anderson describes the paradoxical ideological framework that helped (along with sheer coercion) nurture incoherence of the type found in the program notes: "In the USSR . . . Stalin's victory within the CPSU, based on the promise that it would be possible to build 'socialism in one country,' crystallized a new form of nationalism, specific to the autocracy rapidly being constructed by the Soviet Union. In short order the activities of the Third International were utterly subordinated to the interests of the Soviet state, as Stalin interpreted them. The upshot was the arresting phenomenon, without equivalent before or since, of an internationalism equally deep and deformed, at once rejecting any loyalty to its own country and displaying a limitless loyalty to another state. Its epic was played out by the International Brigades of the Spanish Civil War, shadowed by Comintern emissaries . . . recruited from across all Europe and the Americas. With its mixture of heroism and cynicism, selfless solidarity and murderous terror, this was an internationalism perfected and perverted as never before" ("Internationalism," 15).

43. See Chukovskii, *Poet-Anarkhist Uot Uitman*.

44. Petrovskaia, *"Khizhina diadi Toma."* For a comparison of *Uncle Tom* with *Native Son*, see Abramov, "Syn Diadi Toma."

45. See Clark, *Moscow the Fourth Rome*, 108, 178.

46. Bicher-Stou, *Khizhina diadi Toma* (1941), 372.

47. In Stowe, from "My father, you know" (231) to "down in earth's dust in practice" (240).

48. Kornej Chukovskij, "Bicher-Stou i ee kniga (1811–1896)," in *Sobranie sochinenij v shesti tomakh*, 3:815–33, here 830.

49. Ibid., 827.

50. Ibid.

51. Chukovskij, *Dnevnik, 1930–1969*, 125. The comment suggests that Chukovsky may have tried to publish another version of the piece earlier, probably in the early 1930s, during the fierce war against "formalism" and "idea-lessness."

Chapter 4. Uncle Tom, Cold Warrior

1. Bicher-Stou, *Khizhina diadi Toma*, ed. L. Chumakova, intro. Kornej Chukovskij (Sverdlovsk: Sverdlovskoe Oblastnoe Gosudarstvennoe Izdatel'stvo, 1950), 15–16.

2. I have been unable to find any wartime Soviet edition of *Uncle Tom's Cabin*, unfortunately.

3. Bicher-Stou, *Khizhina diadi Toma ili zhizn' negrov v Amerike.*

4. Ibid., 416–17.

5. Etkind, *Notes of a Non-Conspirator,* 129. The anticosmopolitan campaign seems to have emerged in part as a reaction to the founding of the State of Israel in 1948, met enthusiastically by most Soviet Jews (and initially by the Soviet government as well): suddenly, Jews had a "homeland" and therefore could be traitors. On the campaign, see Nadzhafov, *Stalin i kosmopolitizm;* Slezkine, *Jewish Century,* 297–301.

6. Etkind, *Notes of a Non-Conspirator,* 132.

7. Suny, *Soviet Experiment,* 365. Etkind taught again in Leningrad from 1952 until his departure from the USSR in 1974.

8. Reprinted in Bicher Stou, *Khizhina diadi Toma* [E. L. Voinich, *Ovod*], 5.

9. Georgi Derluguian's phrase in "Recasting Russia," 30.

10. In Mikhalkov, *Sergej Mikhalkov,* 190.

11. The script was released by a major publishing house in Moscow in 1948 (Brushtejn, *Khizhina diadi Toma* [1948]); a translation appeared in Bulgaria the same year (Brushtejn, *Chicho Tomovata Kolina*).

12. A culminating moment was the presentation to the United Nations of the "We Charge Genocide" petition in 1951; see Duberman, *Paul Robeson,* 398.

13. Turkov, *Ot desiati do devianosta,* 68. One undated postwar redaction of the script, however, indicates that a character (derived from Stowe's *Dred*) named Clayton—an abolitionist engineer who teaches slaves both literacy and revolutionary thought and thus functions like the familiar "party commissar" figure from classic works of socialist realism (such as Furmanov in the film *Chapaev* [1934])—steals the finale from Legree, telling the villain that he "will never rule the world" (RGALI, f. 2546, op. 1, d. 4, l. 168). Clayton appears in Brushtein's final, 1967 version as well, though he is not given the last word.

14. Brushtein, *Khizhina diadi Toma* (1967), 77.

15. See Kruk, *Last Days of the Jerusalem of Lithuania,* xxvi–xxxviii, xliv, 53, 67, 80, 163.

16. Bromwich, "Introduction," xxiv.

17. Brushtein did write movingly if briefly about the death of her father at the hands of Fascists, without mentioning the Jewish Holocaust, in the fourth chapter of *Doroga ukhodit v dal'* (1955) and the seventeenth chapter of *V rassvetnyj chas* (1958), the first two volumes of her well-known autobiographical trilogy.

18. Stowe, *Uncle Tom's Cabin* (1961), viii.

19. See McLaren, *Langston Hughes,* 129–31.

20. Stowe, *Uncle Tom's Cabin* (1952), n.p. Hughes's relationship to the novel seems to have been truly complex and mutable: see Reynolds, *Mightier than the Sword,* 259; and Peabody, "Strategies of Visual Intervention." The earliest American preface I have read arguing that "the war brought an end to slavery, but . . . solved nothing so far as the Negro's position in American society was concerned" is Philip Van Doren Stern's in Stowe, *Annotated Uncle Tom's Cabin,*

here 34. But see also Claire Parfait's discussion of Kenneth S. Lynn's introduction to a 1962 Harvard University Press edition in *Publishing History of Uncle Tom's Cabin*, 187–88.

21. From the introduction by N. Sergeeva in Bicher-Stou, *Khizhina diadi Toma* (1955), 7.

22. From the afterword by Aleksandr Chirkov in Bicher-Stou, *Khizhina diadi Toma* (1981), 468.

23. From the introduction by N. Sergeeva in Bicher-Stou, *Khizhina diadi Toma* (1955), 9.

24. Quotation from the back cover of the 2000 "ABC" edition; see note 26 below.

25. Bicher-Stou, *Khizhina diadi Toma*, ed. M. Lorie (1950). Volzhina was also a major translator of the works of Jack London and Sir Arthur Conan Doyle, among others.

26. Bicher-Stou, *Khizhina diadi Toma* (2000). This edition had a print run of ten thousand copies.

27. For the worship scene, see Bicher-Stou, *Khizhina diadi Toma*, ed. M. Lorie (1950), 43.

28. Ibid., 222. The cut runs from (in the original) "The capitalist and aristocrat" to "will not be affected by that."

29. Ibid., 355.

30. Bicher-Stou, *Khizhina diadi Toma* (1977).

31. At least one more edition identical to this one appeared in 1981 (Bicher-Stou, *Khizhina diadi Toma*, trans. Nataliia Volzhina) with a run of two hundred thousand copies.

32. By the early 1960s, teaching guides focusing on Stowe for instructors in high schools and universities were being published: see Ustenko, *Abolitsionistskie Romany Bicher-Stou*; Tugusheva, *Roman*. The latter book is a wide-ranging study of African American responses to Stowe as well and includes discussions of novelists like Ralph Ellison and critics like Barbara Christian.

33. Its immediate predecessor was evidently Harry A. Pollard's 1927 *Uncle Tom's Cabin*, the most elaborate of a large number of silent adaptations of the book. Radványi's film was shot mainly in Yugoslavia and was distributed in its full 70 mm glory in France, Germany, Italy, Yugoslavia, Argentina, Sweden, and many other countries. For more information on the technically innovative filming of Radványi's *Uncle Tom*, see the fascinating essay by Christian Appelt, "Dream Journeys."

34. The film's presentation of slave resistance, or nonresistance, may have also irritated some viewers, Soviet or otherwise. It does conclude with a fiery slave revolt, but Gossett (following Phyllis Klotman) suggests, convincingly in my view, that Radványi might have included the revolt "to avoid the charge that the film portrayed blacks as excessively meek," which in many ways it does (Gossett, *Uncle Tom's Cabin and American Culture*, 405). Legree's property

is destroyed in the film, but this seems a mild punishment relative to his crimes, and he remains alive, free, and intact at the end.

35. In the film, St. Clare chooses to free his slaves on Independence Day, after Eva's death and in response to her dying request. There was considerable interest in the assassination and its mysteries in the USSR. An excerpt from Thomas G. Buchanan's 1964 *Who Killed Kennedy?* appeared in a major Soviet literary journal soon after its American publication (B'iukenen, "Kto ubil Kennedi?"). One wonders whether Legree's ruse in the film (i.e., blaming the murder on the black waiter) was not read in the USSR in relation to the frequent association of Lee Harvey Oswald with Communism.

36. On those more scandalous potential attractions, see Noble, *Masochistic Pleasures of Sentimental Literature*; and Greven, *Men beyond Desire*. The film can be watched in close to its entirety, with a Spanish overdub, at http://www .youtube.com/watch?v=zLzJKPXpLE (multiple files), and was recently released on DVD in Germany (without, alas, English subtitles). In keeping with the great tradition of *Uncle Tom détournement*, Radványi's *Tom* was purchased for distribution by the famous US exploitation film entrepreneur Kroger Babb, trimmed from around 170 to fewer than 120 minutes (mainly by ruthless cutting and removing the prologue and the admittedly superfluous sections with Miss Ophelia and Topsy, the latter an androgynous boy in Radványi's film), and at some point released on video under the Hallmark imprint. (Babb's version is the one discussed by David Reynolds in *Mightier than the Sword*, 238–39 and 261–62.) This condensation was in turn rereleased theatrically by Charles E. Johnson as *Cassy* in 1975, and still later by Samuel Sherman, who added a separate narrative line involving slave traders, rape, interracial romance and a culminating scene of slave vengeance (shot by exploitation legend Al Adamson) for a version titled variously *Uncle Tom's Cabin*, *White Trash Woman*, and *Cry Sweet Revenge* (1977; see http://www.youtube.com/watch?v=VlcuzmLHMY).

37. This was a double edition including *The Scarlet Letter*: Nataniel Gotorn [Nathaniel Hawthorne], *Alaia Bukva* [*The Scarlet Letter*] Bicher-Stou, *Khizhina diadi Toma* (1990). Nikoliukin, who wrote the introduction, is best known as a scholar of American-Russian literary relations and as the general editor of the works of Russian religious thinker V. V. Rozanov (1856–1919).

38. Ibid., 15.

Coda: Tom, Meet Scarlett

1. The new translation is Bicher-Stou, *Khizhina diadi Toma* (2001); it appeared again in 2004 and 2009. In 2005 and 2009, the St. Petersburg publisher "The Bible for All" republished *Khizhina diadi Toma: Povest' iz zhizni unizhennykh* (1909). Judging by prefaces and blurbs, my sense is that the sheer Bible-centeredness of Stowe's novel, rather than any moral teachings to be derived from the actions of Uncle Tom or other characters, has made it attractive to at least some Christian readers in Russia today.

2.   For a brief account of Mitchell in a 1946 Union of Soviet Writers dossier on American authors, see RGALI f. 631, op. 14, d. 1113, l. 15. On *Gone with the Wind* in the context of the historical novel, see Anderson, "From Progress to Catastrophe." The earliest Soviet edition was Margaret Mitchell, *Unesennye vetrom*, 2 vols., trans. T. Ozerskaia, intro. P. Palievskij (Moscow: Khudozhest-vennaia Literatura, 1982).

3.   "The depiction of plantation Georgia in *Gone with the Wind* is romantic, uncritical, eulogistic. Slavery is a benevolent institution, only poor whites and Yankee overseers are ever immoral or ambitious, life is beautiful, Eden is retold. . . . [Mitchell] accepts uncritically all the folklore of Reconstruction, depicts the Ku Klux Klan as a noble institution of the best people chiefly concerned with discouraging black sexual assault upon white women, portrays Reconstruction government as being made up exclusively of scheming Carpetbaggers and deluded blacks" (Rubin, "Scarlett O'Hara," 94). On Soviet rejection of the novel as "popular fiction," see Tlostanova, "Russian 'Fate' of Southern Letters," esp. 42.

4.   Lovell, *Russian Reading Revolution*, 194. Victor Fleming's 1939 film has, of course, also become a Russian favorite.

5.   On Mitchell's contempt for Stowe's novel, see Reynolds, *Mightier than the Sword*, 253. On Cartland's popularity, see Lovell, *Russian Reading Revolution*, 88. Historical fictions by writers as different as Leo Tolstoy, Mikhail Sholokhov, and Valentin Pikul' were among the most-read works during Soviet times.

6.   Mitchell, *Unesennye vetrom* (2002).

7.   See P. Palievskij's introduction to the 1982 *Unesennye vetrom*, 1:3–15. Lovell makes the point very well: "The key to the broad appeal of *Gone with the Wind* was that it cut across accepted generic boundaries—it had something of the [woman's novel], the [adventure novel], and the historical epic. It could therefore be read by men *and* women, the educated elite and the lower strata of the ['mass intelligentsia']" (*Russian Reading Revolution*, 194).

8.   Rubin, "Scarlett O'Hara," 96.

9.   See T. Komarovskaia, "Kniga o krushenii odnoj tsivilizatsii" [A book about the fall of one civilization], in Mitchell, *Unesennye vetrom*, trans. T. Ozerskaia (Minsk: Belorusskaia Sovetskaia Entsiklopediia, 1991), 1:3–10; and E. Stetsenko, "Margaret Mitchell i ee roman *Unesennye vetrom*," in Mitchell, *Unesennye vetrom*, trans. T. Kudriavtseva (Moscow: Dom, 1991), 2:488–95.

10.   "In just five years, from 1990 to 1994, the mortality rate among Russian men soared—in peacetime—by 32 per cent, and their average life-expectancy plummeted to under 58 years, below that of Pakistan. By 2003, the population had fallen by more than five million in a decade, and is currently losing 750,000 lives a year. When Yeltsin took power, the total population of Russia was just under 150 million. By 2050, according to official projections, it will be just over 100 million. So many were not undone by Stalin himself" (Anderson, "Russia's Managed Democracy," here citing http://www.lrb.co.uk/v29/n02/perry-anderson/russias-managed-democracy).

Conclusion

   1. Lovell, *Russian Reading Revolution*, 158.

   2. Acton, "Revolutionaries and Dissidents," 162.

   3. My historical scheme is much influenced by philosopher Étienne Balibar's "threefold meaning of universality," as discussed in his essay "Ambiguous Universality": "*universality as reality*," which involves "a process which creates a single 'world' by multiplying the interdependencies between the units—be they economic, political, or cultural—that form the network of social activities today," through the agency of markets and media, or (for us) capitalism *tout court*, with its political supports and media forms; "*universality as fiction*," or "the kind of universality which was involved in the constitution of social *hegemonies*, and therefore always based upon the existence of state institutions, be they traditional and religious, or modern and secular"; and "*universality as a symbol (or an ideal)*," a "subversive element" that "goes beyond any institutional citizenship, by posing the infinite question of equality *and* liberty together, or the impossibility of actually achieving freedom *without* equality, or equality *without* liberty" ("Ambiguous Universality," in *Politics and the Other Scene*, 146–76; here 170–73). On the emergence of entrepreneurship, see the works by Brooks, Lovell, and Rejtblat already cited, as well as Rieber, *Merchants and Entrepreneurs in Imperial Russia*, esp. 133–257. As far as "universality as ideal" goes in the Russian context, Alexander Radishchev's *Journey from St. Petersburg to Moscow* (1790) would be an early landmark; the present book has mapped out numerous others.

   4. On racism as a form of universalism or "supranationalism," see Étienne Balibar, "Racism and Nationalism," in Balibar and Wallerstein, *Race, Nation, Class*, 37–67, esp. 61–62.

   5. Perhaps the main spaces of political conflict where the interactions between the "universalities" of capital-media, nation, and equalibertarian struggle have encountered the most intractable blockages in recent years are, on one side, debates over "humanitarian intervention" (in the ex-Yugoslavia, Iraq, and very recently Syria, among other places), and debates about migrant labor, on the other; on the latter, see below.

   6. "Real universality is a stage in history where, for the first time, 'humankind' as a single web of interrelationships is no longer an ideal or utopian notion but an actual condition for every individual; nevertheless, far from representing a situation of mutual recognition, it actually coincides with a generalized pattern of conflicts, hierarchies and exclusions. It is not even a situation in which individuals communicate at least virtually with each other, but much more one where global communications networks provide every individual with a distorted image or a stereotype of all the others, either as 'kin' or 'aliens,' thus raising gigantic obstacles to any dialogue. 'Identities' are less isolated *and* more incompatible, less univocal *and* more antagonistic" (Balibar, "Ambiguous Universality," 154–55).

7. See Clément, *Les Ouvriers Russes dans la Tourmente*; Buchanan, "Undefended—Russia's Migrant Workers"; Schwirtz, "For Russia's Migrants"; and T. Wood, "Collapse as Crucible."

8. "The Man That Was a Thing" is the novel's original subtitle.

9. See Balibar's great essay on this topic, "What Is a Border?" in *Politics and the Other Scene*, 75–86.

Bibliography

Archives Consulted

All archival materials consulted during research for this book are located in the Russian State Archive of Literature and Art in Moscow (Rossisskij Gosudarstvennyj Arkhiv Literatury i Iskusstva; here abbreviated RGALI); archive numbers are abbreviated "f." (fond).

RGALI f. 631 (Union of Soviet Writers, Foreign Commission for the United States of America)
RGALI f. 2546 (Aleksandra Iakovlevna Brushtejn)
RGALI f. 3102 (Vladimir Germanovich Lidin)

Published Sources

In Russian, "Stowe" is normally (though not always) referred to as "Beecher-Stowe" ("Bicher-Stou"); thus, the Russian editions of her works are to be found here under "B." Editions of *Uncle Tom's Cabin* are arranged chronologically according to publication date rather than alphabetically.

Abramov, A. "Syn diadi Toma." *Literaturnaia Gazeta* 47 (8 September 1940): 3.
Acton, Edward. "Revolutionaries and Dissidents: The Role of the Russian Intellectual in the Downfall of Tsarism and Communism." In *Intellectuals in Politics: From the Dreyfus Affair to Salman Rushdie*, edited by Jeremy Jennings and Anthony Kemp-Welch, 149–68. London: Routledge, 1997.
———. *Russia: The Tsarist and Soviet Legacy.* 2nd ed. London: Longman, 1995.
Alexandrov, Vladimir. *The Black Russian.* New York: Atlantic Monthly Press, 2013.

Ammons, Elizabeth, ed. *Harriet Beecher Stowe's Uncle Tom's Cabin: A Casebook.* New York: Oxford University Press, 2007.

Anderson, Perry. "From Progress to Catastrophe." *London Review of Books* 33, no. 15 (28 July 2011): 24–28.

———. "Internationalism: A Breviary." *New Left Review* [new series] 14 (March–April 2002): 5–25.

———. "Russia's Managed Democracy." *London Review of Books* 29, no. 2 (25 January 2007): 3–12.

Andreevskij, I. E., et al., eds. *Entsiklopedicheskij Slovar'* [Brockhaus-Efron]. Vol. 4. St. Petersburg: I. A. Efron, 1891.

Anisimov, I. I., et al., eds. *Tolstoj i zarubezhnyj mir (Literaturnoe Nasledstvo 75).* Vol. 1. Moscow: Nauka, 1965.

Anuchin, D. N. *A. S. Pushkin: Antropologicheskij eskiz.* Moscow: Russkie Vedomosti, 1899.

Appelt, Christian. "Dream Journeys: The M.C.S.-70 Process and European Cinema of the 1960s." http://www.in70mm.com/news/2009/mcs_70 /english/index.htm.

Baldwin, James. "Everybody's Protest Novel." *Partisan Review* 16 (June 1949): 578–85.

———. *Notes of a Native Son.* New York: Beacon Press, 1955.

Baldwin, Kate A. *Beyond the Color Line and the Iron Curtain: Reading Encounters between Black and Red, 1922–1963.* Durham, NC: Duke University Press, 2002.

Balibar, Étienne. *Politics and the Other Scene.* Translated by Christine Jones, James Swenson, and Chris Turner. London: Verso, 2007.

Balibar, Étienne, and Immanuel Wallerstein. *Race, Nation, Class: Ambiguous Identities.* Balibar translated by Chris Turner. London: Verso, 1991.

Balukhatyj, S., et al., eds. *Russkie pisateli o literature.* Vol. 1. Leningrad: Sovetskij Pisatel', 1939.

Bennett, Tony. "Texts in History: The Determinations of Readings and Their Texts." In *Reception Study: From Literary Theory to Cultural Studies*, edited by James L. Machor and Philip Goldstein, 61–74. New York: Routledge, 2001.

Bicher-Stou, Garriet [Beecher Stowe, Harriet]. *Begletsy: Epizody iz romana "Khizhina diadi Toma."* Adaptation by N. Moguchij. Moscow: Molodaia Gvardiia, 1930.

———. *Diadia Tom, ili zhizn' negrov-rabov v Amerike.* Adapted and abridged by M. F. Butovich. St. Petersburg, 1867.

———. "Khizhina diadi Toma." Published in four installments in *Russkij Vestnik* 12, no. 12; 13, no. 3 (December 1857–March 1858).

———. *Khizhina diadi Toma.* Translated by P. Novosil'skij et al. St. Petersburg: Tipografiia glavnogo shtaba ego Imperatorskago Velichestva po voenno-uchebnym zavedeniiam, 1858.

————. *Khizhina diadi Toma.* 2nd ed. St. Petersburg: D. F. Fedorov, 1871.

————. *Khizhina diadi Toma ili zhizn' sredi rabov.* Translated by E. Landini. St. Petersburg: D. D. Fedorov, 1883.

————. *Khizhina diadi Toma, ili belye i chernye.* Moscow: Narodnaia Biblioteka, 1884.

————. *Khizhina diadi Toma.* Moscow: I. D. Sytin, 1894.

————. *Khizhina diadi Toma ili belye i chernye.* 5th ed. Moscow: I. N. Kushnerev [in the "People's Library of V. N. Marakuev"], 1895.

————. *Khizhina diadi Toma.* Translated by Z. N. Zhuravskaia. St. Petersburg: O. N. Popova, 1898.

————. *Khizhina diadi Toma.* Translated by E.B. Edited and with an afterword ["Osvoboditeli chernykh rabov"] by I. Gorbunov-Posadov. Moscow: I. D. Sytin, 1902.

————. *Khizhina diadi Toma ili kak negry zhili v nevole.* [*Yasnaya Polyana* ed.] St. Petersburg: Obshchestvennaia Pol'za, 1903.

————. *Khizhina diadi Toma.* Translated by L. A. Murakhina. Moscow: I. D. Sytin, 1908.

————. *Khizhina diadi Toma ili belye i chernye.* Moscow: E. Konovalov, 1910.

————. *Khizhina diadi Toma.* Translated by L. A. Murakhina. 3rd ed. Moscow: I. D. Sytin, 1912.

————. *Khizhina diadi Toma.* Translated by A. M. Vit. Moscow: I. Knebel', 1916.

————. *Khizhina diadi Toma.* Moscow: I. D. Sytin, 1916.

————. *Khizhina diadi Toma.* Moscow: I. D. Sytin, 1917.

————. *Khizhina diadi Toma.* Adapted for children by V. I. Pavlov. Odessa: Odespoligraf, 1925.

————. *Khizhina diadi Toma.* Adapted by E. N. Vinogradskaia. Moscow: Gosudarstvennoe Izdatel'stvo, 1925.

————. *Khizhina diadi Toma: Epizody iz romana.* Adapted by A. Dejch. Moscow: Ogonek, 1928.

————. *Khizhina diadi Toma.* Edited and abridged by M. Leonti'eva. 2nd ed. Odessa: Odespoligraf, 1928.

————. *Khizhina diadi Toma.* Adapted by E. N. Vinogradskaia. Moscow: Gosudarstvennoe Izdatel'stvo, 1928.

————. *Khizhina diadi Toma.* Translated (abridged) by N. and M. Chukovskij. Edited and introduced by Kornej Chukovskij. Illustrated by B. Bekhteev. Moscow: Detskaia Literatura, 1941.

————. *Khizhina diadi Toma ili zhizn' negrov v Amerike.* Edited and adapted by V. S. Val'dman. Afterword by E. Etkind. Leningrad: Leningradskoe Gazetno-zhurnal'noe i Knizhnoe Izdatel'stvo, 1949.

————. *Khizhina diadi Toma.* Edited by L. Chumakova. Introduced by Kornej Chukovskij. Sverdlovsk: Sverdlovskoe Oblastnoe Gosudarstvennoe Izdatel'stvo, 1950.

———. *Khizhina diadi Toma*. Edited by M. Lorie. Translated (abridged) by N. Volzhina. Introduced by N. Sergeeva. Illustrated by S. Prusov. Moscow: Detskaia Literatura, 1950.

———. *Khizhina diadi Toma*. Translated by N. Volzhina. Introduced by N. Sergeeva. Moscow: Detskaia Literatura, 1955.

———. *Khizhina diadi Toma*. Edited by A. Murik. Translated by N. Volzhina. Illustrated by Yu. Ignat'ev. Moscow: Khudozhestvennaia Literatura, 1977.

———. *Khizhina diadi Toma*. Translated by Nataliia Volzhina. Introduced by Aleksandr Chirkov. Kiev: Veselka, 1981.

———. *Khizhina diadi Toma* [with Nataniel Gotorn (Nathaniel Hawthorne), *Alaia Bukva* (*The Scarlet Letter*)]. Translated by N. Volzhina. Introduced by A. Nikoliukin. Moscow: Khudozhestvennaia Literatura, 1990.

———. *Khizhina diadi Toma* [with E. L. Voinich, *Ovod*]. Translated by N. A. Volzhina. Introduced by B. Polevoj. Moscow: Terra, 1994.

———. *Khizhina diadi Toma*. Translated by N. Volzhina. Illustrated by N. Tseitlin. St. Petersburg: Azbuka, 2000.

———. *Khizhina diadi Toma*. Translated by A. E. Polozova. Moscow: Eksmo, 2001. Republished in 2004 and 2009.

———. *Khizhina diadi Toma: Povest' iz zhizni unizhennykh*. [Republication of *Khizhina diadi Toma: Povest' iz zhizni unizhennykh*, translated by A. A. Ragozina (St. Petersburg: P. V. Lukovinkov, 1909).] St. Petersburg: Bibliia dlia vsekh, 2005. Republished in 2009.

Birdoff, Harry. *The World's Greatest Hit: Uncle Tom's Cabin*. New York: S. V. Vanni, 1947.

B'iukenen, Tomas Dzh. [Buchanan, Thomas G.]. "Kto ubil Kennedi?" *Inostrannaia Literatura* 9 (1964): 231–47.

Blakely, Allison. *Russia and the Negro: Blacks in Russian History and Thought*. Washington, DC: Howard University Press, 1986.

Blum, Jerome. *Lord and Peasant in Russia from the Ninth to the Nineteenth Century*. New York: Atheneum, 1966.

Boym, Svetlana. *Death in Quotation Marks: Cultural Myths of the Modern Poet*. Cambridge, MA: Harvard University Press, 1991.

Brewster, Dorothy. *East-West Passage: A Study in Literary Relationships*. London: George Allen and Unwin, 1954.

Briantsev, A. A. *Khudozhnik v teatre dlia detej (V. I. Bejer)*. Leningrad: OSTI, 1927.

Brodhead, Richard H. *Cultures of Letters: Scenes of Reading and Writing in Nineteenth-Century America*. Chicago: University of Chicago Press, 1993.

Bromwich, David. Introduction. In *Uncle Tom's Cabin or, Life among the Lowly*, by Harriet Beecher Stowe, ix–xxv. Cambridge, MA: Belknap Press of Harvard University Press, 2009.

Brooks, Jeffrey. *When Russia Learned to Read: Literacy and Popular Literature, 1861–1917*. Evanston, IL: Northwestern University Press, 2003.

Brown, Gillian. *Domestic Individualism: Imagining Self in Nineteenth-Century America*. Berkeley: University of California Press, 1990.

Brushtejn, A[leksandra]. "Bicher-Stou." *V mire knig* 6 (June 1961): 31–32.

―――. *Chicho Tomovata Kolina*. Sofia: Prevela El. Kostova, 1948.

―――. *Doroga ukhodit v dal'. . . . Trilogiia*. Kishinev: Literatura Artistike, 1987.

―――. *Khizhina diadi Toma*. Moscow: Iskusstvo, 1948.

―――. *Khizhina diadi Toma: Drama A. Brushtejn po motivam proizvedenij Bicher Stou*. Moscow: Otdel rasprostranenij dramaticheskikh proizvedenij VUOAP [Vsesoiuznoe upravlenie po okhrane avtorskikh prav], 1967.

Buchanan, Jane. "Undefended—Russia's Migrant Workers." *Open Democracy Russia* (18 March 2009). http://www.opendemocracy.net/article/email /russia-s-undefendedmigrant-workers.

Buell, Lawrence. "Harriet Beecher Stowe and the Dream of the Great American Novel." In Weinstein, *Cambridge Companion to Harriet Beecher Stowe*, 190–202.

Burbank, Jane. *Intelligentsia and Revolution: Russian Views of Bolshevism, 1917–1922*. New York: Oxford University Press, 1986.

Burbank, Jane, and Frederick Cooper. *Empires in World History: Power and the Politics of Difference*. Princeton, NJ: Princeton University Press, 2010.

Chartier, Roger. *The Order of Books: Readers, Authors and Libraries in Europe between the Fourteenth and Eighteenth Centuries*. Translated by Lydia G. Cochrane. Cambridge: Polity Press, 1994.

Chasles, Philarète. *Études contemporaines: Voyages, philosophie et beaux-Arts*. Paris: Amyot, 1866.

Chekhov, Anton. *A Life in Letters*. Edited by Rosamund Bartlett. Translated by Rosamund Bartlett and Anthony Phillips. London: Penguin Books, 2004.

Chekhov, N. V., ed. *Detskaia literatura*. Moscow: Pol'za, 1909.

Cherkasov, N. K. *Zapiski sovetskogo aktera*. Moscow: Iskusstvo, 1953.

Chernyshevskij, Nikolaj. *Polnoe sobranie sochinenij*. Edited by N. Chernyshev-skaia et al. Moscow: Khudozhestvennaia Literatura, 1950.

―――. *What Is to Be Done? Tales about New People*. Translated by Benjamin R. Tucker. Edited by Ludmilla B. Turkevich. Introduced by E. H. Carr. New York: Vintage Books, 1961.

Christian, David. "Inner Eurasia as a Unit of World History." *Journal of World History* 5, no. 2 (Fall 1994): 173–212.

Chukovskij, Kornej. *Dnevnik, 1930–1969*. Edited by E. T. Chukovskaia. Moscow: Sovremennyj Pisatel', 1994.

―――. *Poet-anarkhist Uot Uitman: Perevod v stikhakh i kharakteristika*. St. Peters-burg: Vol'naia Tipografiia, 1907.

―――. *Sobranie sochinenij v shesti tomakh*. Edited by S. Krasnova. Moscow: Khudozhestvennaia Literatura, 1966.

Clark, Katerina. "Little Heroes and Big Deeds: Literature Responds to the First Five-Year Plan." In *Cultural Revolution in Russia, 1928–1931*, edited by Sheila Fitzpatrick et al., 189–206. Bloomington: Indiana University Press, 1978.

————. *Moscow the Fourth Rome: Stalinism, Cosmopolitanism, and the Evolution of Soviet Culture, 1931–1941*. Cambridge, MA: Harvard University Press, 2011.

————. *The Soviet Novel: History as Ritual*. 3rd ed. Bloomington: Indiana University Press, 2000.

Clément, Karine. *Les Ouvriers Russes dans la Tourmente du Marché 1989–1999: Destruction d'un group social et remobilisations collectives*. Paris: Éditions Syllepse, 2000.

"The 'Crimson Laughter' Terrified the Czar." *New York Times*, 2 July 1905, X1.

Cuevas Diaz, Carmen. "Presencia de Alejandro de Humboldt en la historia de Cuba." In *Alexander von Humboldt und das neue Geschichtsbild von Lateinamerika*, edited by Michael Zeuske and Bernd Schröter, 234–47. Leipzig: Leipziger Universitätsverlag, 1992.

Derluguian, Georgi. "Recasting Russia." *New Left Review*, 2nd ser., 12 (November–December 2001): 5–31.

Dobrenko, Evgeny. *The Making of the State Reader: Social and Aesthetic Contexts of the Reception of Soviet Literature*. Translated by Jesse M. Savage. Stanford, CA: Stanford University Press, 1997.

Dow, Roger. "Seichas: A Comparison of Pre-Reform Russia and the Ante-Bellum South." *Russian Review* 7, no. 1 (Autumn 1947): 3–15.

Drejden, S. D., ed. *Nikolaj Cherkasov*. Moscow: Vserossijskoe Teatral'noe Obshchestvo, 1976.

Duberman, Martin. *Paul Robeson*. New York: New Press, 1995.

Engelstein, Laura. "Print Culture and the Transformation of Imperial Russia: Three New Views." *Comparative Studies in Society and History* 31, no. 4 (October 1989): 784–90.

Etkind, Efim. *Notes of a Non-Conspirator*. Translated by Peter France. Oxford: Oxford University Press, 1978.

Fedorov, M. *Khizhina diadi Toma*. Moscow: S. O. Razsokhin, 1890.

Fet, A. A. "Nashi Korni." In *A. A. Fet: Poet i myslitel'*, edited by E. N. Lebedev, 171–234. Moscow: Nasledie, 1999.

Field, Daniel. *The End of Serfdom: Nobility and Bureaucracy in Russia, 1855–1861*. Cambridge, MA: Harvard University Press, 1976.

Fisher, Philip. *Hard Facts: Setting and Form in the American Novel*. New York: Oxford University Press, 1985.

Fitzpatrick, Sheila. *The Cultural Front: Power and Culture in Revolutionary Russia*. Ithaca, NY: Cornell University Press, 1992.

————. *Stalin's Peasants: Resistance and Survival in the Russian Village after Collectivization*. Oxford: Oxford University Press, 1994.

Foote, I. P. *The St. Petersburg Censorship Committee, 1828–1905*. Oxford: Oxford University Press, 1992.

Friche. V. M., et al., eds. *Literaturnaia Entsiklopediia*. Vol. 1. Moscow: Izdatel'stvo Kommunisticheskoj Akademii, 1930.

Frierson, Cathy A. *Peasant Icons: Representations of Rural People in Late Nineteenth-Century Russia.* New York: Oxford University Press, 1993.

Friol, Roberto. *En la cabaña del Tío Tom.* Havana: Departamento de Colección Cubana, Biblioteca Nacional José Martí, 1967.

Furnas, J. C. *Goodbye to Uncle Tom.* New York: William Sloan, 1956.

Gertsen [Herzen], Aleksandr. *Sobranie sochinenij v tridtsati tomakh.* Edited by V. A. Putintsev et al. Moscow: Izdatel'stvo Akademii Nauk SSSR, 1957.

Getty, J. Arch, and Oleg V. Naumov. *The Road to Terror: Stalin and the Self-Destruction of the Bolsheviks, 1932–1939.* New Haven, CT: Yale University Press, 1999.

Goldman, Hannah Stern. "American Slavery and Russian Serfdom: A Study in Fictional Parallels." PhD diss., Columbia University, 1955.

Goldstein, Robert Justin. "Fighting French Censorship, 1815–1881." *French Review* 71, no. 5 (April 1998): 785–96.

Golovin, Ivan. *Rovira: Drama v trekh dejstviiakh.* Leipzig: Wolfgang Gerhard, 1858.

———. *Stars and Stripes or American Impressions.* London: W. Freeman and D. Appleton, 1856.

Gor'kij, M. *O detskoj literature, detskom i iunosheskom chtenii.* Moscow: Detskaia Literatura, 1989.

Gossett, Thomas F. *Uncle Tom's Cabin and American Culture.* Dallas: Southern Methodist University Press, 1985.

Greven, David. *Men beyond Desire: Manhood, Sex, and Violation in American Literature.* New York: Palgrave Macmillan, 2005.

Hartman, Saidiya. *Scenes of Subjection: Terror, Slavery, and Self-Making in Nineteenth-Century America.* Oxford: Oxford University Press, 1997.

Hecht, David. "Russian Intelligentsia and American Slavery." *Phylon (1940–56)* 9, no. 3 (3rd qtr., 1948): 265–69.

Hedrick, Joan D. *Harriet Beecher Stowe: A Life.* New York: Oxford University Press, 1994.

Herzberg, Julia. "Onkel Vanjas Hütte: Erzählte Leibeigenschaft in der bäuerlichen Autobiografik des Zarenreichs." *Jahrbücher für Geschichte Osteuropas* 58, no. 1 (2010): 24–51.

Herzberg, Julia, and Christoph Schmidt, eds. *Vom Wir zum Ich: Individuum und Autobiografik im Zarenreich.* Cologne: Böhlau Verlag, 2007.

Hill, Michael Gibbs. *Lin Shu, Inc.: Translation and the Making of Modern Chinese Culture.* New York: Oxford University Press, 2012.

Hochman, Barbara. *Uncle Tom's Cabin and the Reading Revolution: Race, Literacy, Childhood, and Fiction, 1851–1911.* Amherst: University of Massachusetts Press, 2011.

James, Henry. "Ivan Turgéniew." *North American Review* 118, no. 253 (April 1874): 326–56.

Jameson, Fredric. "The Vanishing Mediator; or, Max Weber as Storyteller." In *The Ideologies of Theory*, 309-43. London: Verso, 2008.

Jorgenson, Chester E. *Uncle Tom's Cabin as Book and Legend: A Guide to an Exhibition*. Detroit: Friends of the Detroit Public Library, 1952.

Karajchentseva, S. A. *Russkaia detskaia kniga XVIII-XX vv. (Ocherki evoliutsii repertuara, 1717-1990 gg.)*. Moscow: Moskovskij Gosudarstvennyj Universitet Pechati, 2006.

Kaspin, Albert. "*Uncle Tom's Cabin* and 'Uncle' Akim's Inn: More on Harriet Beecher Stowe and Turgenev." *Slavic and East European Journal* 9, no. 1 (Spring 1965): 47-55.

Katarskij, I. *Dikkens v Rossii*. Moscow: Nauka, 1966.

Kelley, Robin D.G. *Hammer and Hoe: Alabama Communists during the Great Depression*. Chapel Hill: University of North Carolina Press, 1990.

Kelly, Catriona. *Children's World: Growing Up in Russia, 1890-1991*. New Haven, CT: Yale University Press, 2007.

Khomyakov, A. S. *Polnoe sobranie sochinenij*. Moscow: Universitetskaia Tipografiia, 1904.

Klunder, Willard Carl. *Lewis Cass and the Politics of Moderation*. Kent, OH: Kent State University Press, 1996.

Knight, Nathaniel. "Was the Intelligentsia Part of the Nation? Visions of Society in Post-Emancipation Russia." *Kritika: Explorations in Russian and Eurasian History* 7, no. 4 (Fall 2006): 733-58.

Kohn, Denise, Sarah Meer, and Emily B. Todd, eds. *Transatlantic Stowe: Harriet Beecher Stowe and European Culture*. Iowa City: University of Iowa Press, 2006.

Kolchin, Peter. *Unfree Labor: American Slavery and Russian Serfdom*. Cambridge, MA: Belknap Press of Harvard University Press, 1987.

Kolonickij, Boris I. "Les identités de l'intelligentsia russe et l'anti intellectualisme." *Cahiers du Monde Russe* 43 (2002/4): 601-16.

Korf, Baron Nikolai Aleksandrovich. *Nash drug, kniga dlia chteniia v shkole i doma*. St. Petersburg, 1886.

Körner, Axel. "Uncle Tom on the Ballet Stage: Italy's Barbarous America, 1850-1900." *Journal of Modern History* 83 (December 2011): 721-52.

Kruk, Herman. *The Last Days of the Jerusalem of Lithuania: Chronicles from the Vilna Ghetto and the Camps, 1939-1944*. Edited by Benjamin Harshav. Translated by Barbara Harshav. New Haven, CT: Yale University Press, 2002.

Kudriavtseva, E. B. *Dlia serdtsa i razuma: Detskaia literatura v Rossii XVIII v.* St. Petersburg: Nestor-Istoriia, 2010.

Kugushev, Prince G. "Duniasha: Legenda davnikh vremen." *Russkij Vestnik* 12, no. 1 (December 1857): 640-42.

Lemke, Mikhail. "Emigrant Ivan Golovin: Po neizdannym materialam." *Byloe* 5 (1907): 39.

———. *Nikolaevskie Zhandarmy i Literatura 1826-1855 gg*. 2nd ed. St. Petersburg: S. V. Bunin, 1909.

———. *Ocherki po istorii russkoj tsenzury i zhurnalistiki XIX stoletiia.* St. Petersburg: Trud, 1904.

Lenoe, Matthew. *Closer to the Masses: Stalinist Culture, Social Revolution, and Soviet Newspapers.* Cambridge, MA: Harvard University Press, 2004.

Liubashevskij L. [D. Del']. *Rasskazy o teatre i kino.* Leningrad: Iskusstvo, 1964.

Lott, Eric. *Love and Theft: Blackface Minstrelsy and the American Working Class.* New York: Oxford University Press, 1993.

Lovell, Stephen. *The Russian Reading Revolution: Print Culture in the Soviet and Post-Soviet Eras.* New York: St. Martin's Press, 2000.

Lucas, Edith E. *La littérature anti-esclavagiste au dix-neuvième siècle: Étude sur Madame Beecher Stowe et son influence en France.* Paris: E. de Boccard, 1930.

MacKay, John, trans. and ed. *Four Russian Serf Narratives.* Madison: University of Wisconsin Press, 2009.

Maclean, Grace Edith. *Uncle Tom's Cabin in Germany.* Americana Germanica 10. New York: D. Appleton, 1910.

Mamatey, Victor S., and Radomir Luzha, eds. *A History of the Czechoslovak Republic, 1918–1948.* Princeton, NJ: Princeton University Press, 1973.

McLaren, Joseph. *Langston Hughes: Folk Dramatist in the Protest Tradition, 1921–1943.* Introduced by Beth Turner. Afterword by James V. Hatch. Westport, CT: Greenwood Press, 1997.

Meer, Sarah. *Uncle Tom Mania: Slavery, Minstrelsy, and Transatlantic Culture in the 1850s.* Athens: University of Georgia Press, 2005.

Mikhalkov, Sergej. *Sergej Mikhalkov.* Moscow: Sovremennik, 1973.

Miller, Frank J. *Folklore for Stalin: Russian Folklore and Pseudofolklore of the Stalin Era.* Armonk, NY: M. E. Sharpe, 1990.

Mitchell, Margaret. *Unesennye vetrom.* Translated by T. Ozerskaia. Introduced by P. Palievskij. Moscow: Khudozhestvennaia Literatura, 1982.

———. *Unesennye vetrom.* Translated by T. Ozerskaia. Introduced by T. Komarovskaia. Minsk: Belorusskaia Sovetskaia Entsiklopediia, 1991.

———. *Unesennye vetrom.* Translated by T. Kudriatsevaia. Afterword by E. Stetsenko. Moscow: Dom, 1991.

———. *Unesennye vetrom.* Translated by T. A. Kudriavtseva and T. Ozerskaia. Introduced by E. A. Stetsenko. Annotated by A. I. Blejz. Moscow: NF Pushkinskaia Biblioteka, OOO Izdatel'stvo AST, 2002.

Mogil'ner, Marina. *Homo Imperii: Istoriia fizicheskoj antropologii v Rossii (konets XIX–nachalo XX v.).* Moscow: Novoe Literaturnoe Obozrenie, 2008.

Moon, David. *The Abolition of Serfdom in Russia, 1762–1907.* Edinburgh: Longman, 2001.

Morgan, Jo-Ann. *Uncle Tom's Cabin as Visual Culture.* Columbia: University of Missouri Press, 2007.

Morris, Robert C., ed. *Freedmen's Schools and Textbooks.* New York: AMS Press, 1980.

————. *Reading, Riting, and Reconstruction: The Education of Freedmen in the South, 1861–1870*. Chicago: University of Chicago Press, 1981.

Morson, Gary Saul. "What Is the Intelligentsia? Once More, an Old Russian Question." *Academic Questions* 6 (Summer 1993): 20–38.

Müller, Otto Wilhelm. *Intelligencija: Untersuchungen zur Geschichte eines politischen Schlagwortes*. Frankfurt am Main: Athenäum Verlag, 1971.

Nadzhafov, D. G., ed. *Stalin i kosmopolitizm: Dokumenty Agitpropa TsK KPSS 1945–1953*. Moscow: Materik, 2005.

Nathans, Benjamin. *Beyond the Pale: The Jewish Encounter with Late Imperial Russia*. Berkeley: University of California Press, 2002.

Nepomnyashchy, Catharine Theimer, Nicole Svobodny, and Ludmilla A. Trigos, eds. *Under the Sky of My Africa: Alexander Pushkin and Blackness*. Introduced by Henry Louis Gates Jr. Evanston, IL: Northwestern University Press, 2006.

Nikoliukin, A. N. *Literaturnye sviazi Rossii i SSha: Stanovlenie literaturnykh kontaktov*. Moscow: Nauka, 1981.

————, ed. *A Russian Discovery of America*. Translated by Cynthia Carlile and Julius Katzer. Moscow: Progress, 1986.

————, ed. *Vzgliad v istoriiu—vzgliad v budushchee: Russkie i sovetskie pisateli, uchenye, deiateli kul'tury o SSHA*. Moscow: Progress, 1987.

Noble, Marianne. *The Masochistic Pleasures of Sentimental Literature*. Princeton, NJ: Princeton University Press, 2000.

Orlova, R. D. *Garriet Bicher-Stou: Ocherk zhizni i tvorchestva*. Moscow: Prosveshchenie, 1971.

————. *Khizhina, ustoiavshaia stoletie*. Moscow: Kniga, 1975.

P.E. "Pomeshchiki i krest'iane." *Russkij Vestnik* [Sovremennaia letopis'] 19, no. 2 (January 1859): 219–30.

Page, Thomas Nelson. *In Ole Virginia*. New York: Charles Scribner's Sons, 1895.

Parfait, Claire. *The Publishing History of Uncle Tom's Cabin, 1852–2002*. Aldershot, UK: Ashgate, 2007.

Paustovskij, Konstantin. "Novoe amerikanskikh pisatelej [The New Generation of American Writers]." *Vzgliad v istoriiu—vzgliad v budushchee: Russkie i sovetskie pisateli, uchenye, deiateli kul'tury o SSHA*. Edited by A. N. Nikoliukin, 415. Moscow: Progress, 1987.

Peabody, Rebecca. "Strategies of Visual Intervention: Langston Hughes and *Uncle Tom's Cabin*." *Comparative Literature* 62, no. 2 (Spring 2012): 169–91.

Pechat' RSFSR v 1922 godu. Moscow: Gosudarstvennoe Izdatel'stvo, 1924.

Pehle, Walter H., ed. *November 1938: From Reichskristallnacht to Genocide*. Oxford: Berg, 1990.

Petrovskaia, T. "*Khizhina diadi Toma*." *Literaturnaia Gazeta* 5 (5 February 1941): 3.

Pisarev, Dmitry. *Selected Philosophical, Social, and Political Essays*. Translated by R. Dixon. Moscow: Foreign Languages Publishing House, 1958.

Placido, Beniamino. *Due schiavitù: Per un'analisi dell'immaginazione Americana*. Turin: G. Einaudi, 1975.

Portelli, Alessandro. "*Uncle Tom's Cabin* (Harriet Beecher Stowe, United States, 1852)." *The Novel.* Vol. 1, *History, Geography, and Culture.* Edited by Franco Moretti, 805-15. Princeton, NJ: Princeton University Press, 2006.

Programma: Khizhina diadi Toma. Krasnoiarsk: Krasnoyarskij Teatr Dramy im. A. S. Pushkina, 1938.

Pushchin, I. I. *Sochineniia i pis'ma.* Edited by M. P. and S. V. Mironenko. Moscow: Nauka, 2001.

Pyron, Darden Asbury, ed. *Recasting: Gone with the Wind in American Culture.* Miami: University Presses of Florida, 1983.

Razumovsky, Maria. *Marina Tsvetaeva: A Critical Biography.* Translated by Aleksey Gibson. Newcastle upon Tyne: Bloodaxe Books, 1994.

Reiser, S., et al., eds. *Literaturnoe Nasledstvo.* Vols. 53-54. Moscow: Izdatel'stvo Akademii Nauk SSSR, 1949.

Rejtblat, A. I. *Ot Bovy k Bal'montu i drugie raboty po istoricheskoj sotsiologii russkoj literatury.* Moscow: Novoe Literaturnoe Obozrenie, 2009.

Reynolds, David S. *Mightier than the Sword: Uncle Tom's Cabin and the Battle for America.* New York: W. W. Norton, 2011.

Rieber, Alfred J. *Merchants and Entrepreneurs in Imperial Russia.* Chapel Hill: University of North Carolina Press, 1982.

Roach, Joseph. *Cities of the Dead: Circum-Atlantic Performance.* New York: Columbia University Press, 1996.

Rogers, James Allen. "Racism and Russian Revolutionists." *Race & Class* 14, no. 3 (1973): 279-89.

Rogger, Hans. *Russia in the Age of Modernisation and Revolution 1881-1917.* London: Longman, 1983.

Rubin, Louis, Jr. "Scarlett O'Hara and the Two Quentin Compsons." In *Recasting: Gone with the Wind in American Culture,* edited by Darden Asbury Pyron, 81-104. Miami: University Presses of Florida, 1983.

Ruud, Charles A. *Fighting Words: Imperial Censorship and the Russian Press, 1804-1906.* Toronto: University of Toronto Press, 1982.

Saul, Norman E. *Concord and Conflict: The United States and Russia, 1867-1914.* Lawrence: University Press of Kansas, 1996.

———. *Distant Friends: The United States and Russia, 1763-1867.* Lawrence: University Press of Kansas, 1991.

Schwirtz, Michael. "For Russia's Migrants, Economic Despair Douses Flickers of Hope." *New York Times,* 10 February 2009.

Semevskij, V. I. *Krest'ianskij vopros v Rossii v XVIII i pervoj polovine XIX veka.* St. Petersburg: Obshchestvennaia Pol'za, 1888.

Shebunin, A. N. *Nikolaj Ivanovich Turgenev.* Moscow: Gosudarstvennoe Izdatel'stvo, 1925.

Sirotinin, V. S. "Kommunisticheskij terror v Krasnoiarskom krae." http://www.memorial.krsk.ru/Articles/KP/1/06.htm.

Skabichevskij, A. M. *Ocherki istorii russkoj tsenzury (1700-1863 gg.).* St. Petersburg: Obshchestvennaia Pol'za, 1892.

Slezkine, Yuri. *The Jewish Century*. Princeton, NJ: Princeton University Press, 2004.

Smirnov, Nikolai. *"Iasnaia Poliana" L'va Tolstogo*. Tula: Priokskoe Knizhnoe Izdatel'stvo, 1991.

Stanislawski, Michael. *Tsar Nicholas I and the Jews: The Transformation of Jewish Society in Russia, 1825–1855*. Philadelphia: Jewish Publication Society of America, 1983.

Stowe, Harriet Beecher. *La Cabane de l'Oncle Tom ou Les Noirs en Amérique*. Translated by Léon de Wailly and Edmond Texier. 2nd ed. Paris: Perrotin, 1853.

———. *Uncle Tom's Cabin*. Philadelphia: John C. Winston, n.d.

———. *Uncle Tom's Cabin*. Edited by H. E. Marshall. Illustrated by A. S. Forrest. Edinburgh: T. C. Jack, 1904.

———. *Uncle Tom's Cabin*. Introduced by Langston Hughes. New York: Dodd, Mead, 1952.

———. *Uncle Tom's Cabin*. Introduced by Van Wyck Brooks. London: J. M. Dent, 1961.

———. *The Annotated Uncle Tom's Cabin*. Introduced by Philip Van Doren Stern. New York: Paul S. Eriksson, 1964.

———. *Uncle Tom's Cabin*. Edited and introduced by Jean Fagan Yellin. Oxford: Oxford University Press, 1998.

———. *Uncle Tom's Cabin: Authoritative Text, Backgrounds and Contexts, Criticism*. Edited by Elizabeth Ammons. New York: W. W. Norton, 2010.

Sunderland, Willard. "Peasants on the Move: Peasant Resettlement in Imperial Russia, 1805–1830s." *Russian Review* 52 (October 1993): 472–85.

Sundquist, Eric J., ed. *New Essays on Uncle Tom's Cabin*. Cambridge: Cambridge University Press, 1986.

———. "Slavery, Revolution, and the American Renaissance." In *The American Renaissance Reconsidered*, edited by Walter Benn Michaels and Donald E. Pease, 1–33. Baltimore: Johns Hopkins University Press, 1985.

Suny, Ronald Grigor. *The Soviet Experiment: Russia, the USSR, and the Successor States*. New York: Oxford University Press, 1998.

Tlostanova, Madina. "The Russian 'Fate' of Southern Letters, or Southern Fiction and 'Soviet' Diction." *South Atlantic Review* 65, no. 4 (Autumn 2000): 28–50.

Tocqueville, Alexis de. *Democracy in America*. Edited by J. P. Mayer. New York: Harper Collins, 1988.

Tolstoj, Lev [Graf L. N. Tolstoy]. *Azbuka*. St. Petersburg: K. Zamyslovskij, 1872.

———. *Perepiska s russkimi pisateliami*. Edited by S. A. Rozanova. 2nd ed. Moscow: Khudozhestvennaia Literatura, 1978.

———. *Polnoe sobranie sochinenij*. Edited by V. G. Chertkov et al. Moscow: Khudozhestvennaia Literatura, 1937.

———. *Polnoe sobranie sochinenij*. Edited by L. D. Opul'skaia et al. Moscow: Khudozhestvennaia Literatura, 1953.

———. *Tolstoy on Art*. Edited and translated by Aylmer Maude. London: Humphrey Milford and Oxford University Press, 1925.

———. "What Is Art?" In *Complete Works of Count Tolstoy*, translated and edited by Leo Wiener, 22:135–53. Boston: Dana Estes, 1904.

Tompkins, Jane. *Sensational Designs: The Cultural Work of American Fiction, 1790–1860*. New York: Oxford University Press, 1985.

———. "Sentimental Power: *Uncle Tom's Cabin* and Literary History." *Glyph* 2 (1978): 80–102.

Tsvetaeva, Marina. *Selected Poems*. Translated and introduced by Elaine Feinstein. New York: Penguin Books, 1993.

———. *Sobranie sochinenij v semi tomakh*. Edited by Lev Mnukhin. Moscow: Ellis Lak, 1995.

Tugusheva, M. *Roman G. Bicher Stou "Khizhina diadi Toma."* Moscow: Vysshaia Shkola, 1985.

Turgenev, Ivan. *Memoires d'un Seigneur Russe*. Translated by Ernest Charrière. Paris: Hachette, 1854.

———. [Ivan Tourghenief]. "Photographs from Russian Life." *Fraser's Magazine for Town and Country* 50, no. 296 (August 1854): 209–22.

———. *Polnoe sobranie pisem v trinadtsati tomakh*. Edited by B. M. Eikhenbaum et al. Moscow: Izdatel'stvo Akademii Nauk, 1961.

———. *Polnoe sobranie sochinenij v dvadtsati tomakh*. Edited by A. N. Dubovikov et al. Moscow: Izdatel'stvo Akademii Nauk SSSR, 1963.

———. [Ivan Turgenieff]. *Spring Freshets, Smoke and Other Stories*. Translated by Isabel F. Hapgood. New York: Willey, 1904.

———. *Three Novellas*. Translated by Marion Mainwaring. New York: Farrar, Straus and Giroux, 1969.

Turgenev [Tourgueneff], Nikolai. *La Russie et les Russes*. 3 vols. Paris: Comptoir des Imprimeurs-unis, 1847.

———. "Russia and the Russians." In *The Liberty Bell: By Friends of Freedom*, 210–25. Boston: National Anti-Slavery Bazaar, 1853.

Turkov, A. *Ot desiati do devianosta: O tvorchestve A. Ia. Brushtejn*. Moscow: Detskaia Literatura, 1966.

Ushinskij, K. D. *Pedagogicheskie sochineniia v shesti tomakh*. Moscow: Pedagogika, 1988.

Ustenko, G. A. *Abolitsionistskie Romany Bicher-Stou ("Khizhina diadi Toma," "Dred")*. Odessa: Odesskij Gosudarstvennyj Universitet, 1961.

"Vnutrennie partii v Soedinennykh shtatakh." *Russkij Vestnik* [*Sovremennaia letopis'*] 3, no. 1 (May 1856): 1–17.

Warren, Kenneth W. "The Afterlife of *Uncle Tom's Cabin*." In Weinstein, *Cambridge Companion to Harriet Beecher Stowe*, 219–34.

Weeks, Theodore R. *Nation and State in Late Imperial Russia: Nationalism and Russification on the Western Frontier, 1863–1914*. DeKalb: Northern Illinois University Press, 1996.

Weinstein, Cindy, ed. *A Cambridge Companion to Harriet Beecher Stowe.* Cambridge: Cambridge University Press, 2004.

Williams, Heather Andrea. *Self-Taught: African-American Education in Slavery and Freedom.* Chapel Hill: University of North Carolina Press, 2005.

Williams, Linda. *Playing the Race Card: Melodramas of Black and White from Uncle Tom to O. J. Simpson.* Princeton, NJ: Princeton University Press, 2001.

Wilson, Edmund. *Patriotic Gore: Studies in the Literature of the American Civil War.* New York: Farrar, Straus and Giroux, 1962.

Wilson, Forrest. *Crusader in Crinoline: The Life of Harriet Beecher Stowe.* Philadelphia: J.B. Lippincott, 1941.

Wood, Marcus. *Blind Memory: Visual Representations of Slavery in England and America, 1780–1865.* Manchester: Manchester University Press, 2000.

Wood, Tony. "Collapse as Crucible: The Reforging of Russian Society." *New Left Review* 74, n.s. (March–April 2012): 5–38.

"Zagranichnye izvestiia." *Sovremennik* 61, no. 1 (1857): 140–42.

Zorine, Andreï, and Andreï Nemzer. "Les paradoxes de la sentimentalité." In *Livre et lecture en Russie,* edited by Alexandre Stroev, 91–123. Paris: Institut Mémoires de l'édition contemporaine/Maison des science de l'homme, 1996.

Filmography

Onkel Toms Hütte [*Uncle Tom's Cabin*]. Directed by Géza von Radványi. Produced by Aldo von Pinelli. 1965 [released in the USSR in 1966].

Index

abolitionism, 9–10, 16–17, 56, 73, 97, 112n1, 113n10. *See also* serfdom (Russian); slavery (US)

Acton, Edward, 96–97, 134n2

Africa, 7, 100, 125n88

Alcott, Louisa May, 46; *Little Women*, 46

Alexander I (Tsar), 26

Alexander II (Tsar), xiii, 12

Annenkov, Pavel, 37–38. *See also* Turgenev, Ivan

anticosmopolitan campaign, xiv, 82–84, 99, 130n5. *See also* anti-Semitism; Stalin, Joseph

anti-Semitism, xiv, 82–86, 99, 130n5. *See also* anticosmopolitan campaign; fascism; racism

Balázs, Béla, 89. *See also* Radványi, Géza von

Baldwin, James, xiv, 34, 86, 108n12

Balibar, Etienne, 100, 134nn3–4, 134n6, 135n9

Balzac, Honoré, 94

Bejer, V. I., 75, 128n36. *See also* Brushtein, Alexandra

Belinsky, Vissarion, 37, 41, 46, 121n51

Black Pilgrims, xiii, 72, 127n26

Bludova, A. D. (Baroness), 17

Bolsheviks, xiii, 62, 63, 71. *See also* Communist Party (USSR)

Brecht, Bertolt, 6

Brezhnev, Leonid, xiv

Briantsev, Alexander, 74. *See also* Brushtein, Alexandra

Britain, 7, 23–24

Brockhaus-Efron (encyclopedia), 39, 120n26

Bromwich, David, 86, 130n16

Brooks, Van Wyck, 86

Brown v. Board of Education, xiv

Brushtein, Alexandra, 74–77, 84–86, 89, 127n33, 128n34, 128nn36–40, 129n41, 130n11, 130nn13–15. See also *Uncle Tom's Cabin* (stage versions); Vygodsky, Iakov

Brzezinski, Zbigniew, 89

Buell, Lawrence, 35, 119n13, 120n29

Bunin, Ivan, 5

Butovich, Mitrofan Fedorovich, 44–47. *See also* Tolstoy, Leo; *Yasnaya Polyana*

Carroll, Lewis, 80

Carter, Jimmy, 89

Cartland, Barbara, 94, 133n5

Cass, Lewis, 14, 113n14

censorship, 12–14, 27–28, 32–33, 45–46, 64–74, 88–89, 109n16, 112n1, 113n12,

reading practices, 44–62, 87, 110n17, 122nn55–56, 122n58, 122nn60–63, 123n69. *See also* reception (literary)

reception (literary), 8, 37–44, 62–74, 86, 97–101, 109nn14–15, 110n18. *See also* reading practices

Reconstruction (US), xiii, 94

Reikhel', Maria, 14, 22

Revolutions: 1848, 29; 1905 (Russia), xiii; February 1917, xiii, 63; French, 29–30, 97; October 1917, xiii, 10, 63, 92

Richardson, Samuel, 20; *Clarissa*, 20

Ripley, Alexandra, 94; *Scarlett*, 94. *See also* Mitchell, Margaret

Robeson, Paul, 83

Rousseau, Jean-Jacques, 20; *Nouvelle Héloïse*, 20

Rubin, Louis Jr., 94–95, 133n3, 133n8. See also *Gone with the Wind*; Mitchell, Margaret

Russian Messenger (journal), 20, 23, 26–28, 32, 36, 44, 112n4, 117n62

Sand, George, 13, 113n8

San Domingo (Haiti), 30, 59–61

Saxonism, 29, 56, 60. *See also* racism

Schiller, Friedrich von, 40

sentimentalism, 7, 19–20, 23, 46–47, 68, 88, 98, 108n13, 115n39, 116n48

serfdom (Russian), 8–9, 15–27, 79, 112nn3–4, 113n12, 114nn27–31, 115n32, 115nn43–44, 116n46, 116n49, 116n52, 117n62, 118n12, 119nn16–17; aftermath of, 47–48, 50, 56; emancipation, xiii, 8, 14, 26, 33, 44; termination of redemption payments, xiii. *See also* peasants; slavery (US)

Sinyavsky, Andrei, 5, 108n9. *See also* dissidence

slavery (US), 7, 10, 14, 16–21, 33, 44, 50, 65, 72, 79, 108n12, 112n1, 113n14, 114n31, 115n40, 115n45, 116n48, 116n50, 116n52, 117n54, 118n3, 121n50, 123n72,

124n73, 124n81, 130n20. *See also* serfdom (Russian)

Slavophiles, 17–18. *See also* Khomyakov, Aleksei

Smirnov, A., 45–46, 98. *See also* Butovich, Mitrofan Fedorovich; censorship; Tolstoy, Leo

socialist realism, 5, 80, 85

Son of the Fatherland (journal), 26

Soviet Union, xiii, xv, 7–8, 62, 64–65, 71–74, 91–95

Stalin, Joseph, xiii–xiv, 5, 64, 80, 82, 84, 99. *See also* anticosmopolitan campaign; collectivization; First Five-Year Plan; Great Terror

Standard (*National Anti-Slavery Standard*, abolitionist newspaper), 16

Stowe, Harriet Beecher, xiii, 3–5 and *passim*; *Dred*, 26, 85; as exemplar, 36–37, 49–50; "Lady Byron Vindicated," 39; as novelist, 35–36, 39; and Tolstoy, 43–44; and Turgenev, 35–39. *See also* Tolstoy, Leo; Turgenev, Ivan; *Uncle Tom's Cabin* (novel)

Strel'nikov, Nikolai, 75. *See also* Brushtein, Alexandra

Suny, Ronald, 63, 108n9, 126n5

Suttner, Bertha von, 44. *See also* Tolstoy, Leo

Svistunov, P. N., 15

Sytin, Ivan, 48, 52, 54, 57. *See also* Gorbunov-Posadov, Ivan; Tolstoy, Leo

Tesková, Anna, 3. *See also* Tsvetaeva, Marina

Thaw, xiv, 5

Third Congress of Aix-la-Chapelle, 26

Thoreau, Henry David, 91

Tolstoy, Leo, 8, 15, 32, 34, 39–51, 58, 61, 91–92, 98–99, 120nn28–40, 121n41, 122n67, 123n69, 133n5; "Death of Ivan Ilych," 49; "A Landlord's Morning," 41; "Polikushka," 41–42; *Resurrection*, 20; *War*